Portrait of Patriotism
"Washington Crossing the Delaware"

Emanuel Leutze

Portrait of Patriotism

"Washington Crossing the Delaware"

———◆———

ANN HAWKES HUTTON

Illustrated

CHILTON COMPANY—BOOK DIVISION
Publishers
Philadelphia   New York

FIRST EDITION

COPYRIGHT © 1959 BY
ANN HAWKES HUTTON

All Rights Reserved

Published in Philadelphia by Chilton Company
and simultaneously in Toronto, Canada, by Ambassador Books, Ltd.

LIBRARY OF CONGRESS CATALOG CARD NUMBER 59-13779
MANUFACTURED IN THE UNITED STATES OF AMERICA

Dedication

To my husband—with love and appreciation for his always helpful interest.

Preface

America's best known "Portrait of Patriotism" dramatizes the most critical hour in her struggle for independence and emphasizes the courageous leadership of George Washington. The crossing of the Delaware River on Christmas night, 1776, inspired many a nineteenth-century youth with zeal for his freedom-loving country. One of those deeply impressed by its significance was young Abraham Lincoln.

Another was the gifted American artist, Emanuel Leutze. He was so convinced that this momentous event provided the best possible character study of George Washington that he used it as the historical setting for his portrait of the Commander in Chief.

Leutze was an ambitious young American. He set a goal to be a successful painter and worked conscientiously toward that aim. He studied constantly and worked faithfully. His work idealized the history of his country and its great men. He admired Washington and his courageous leadership, and by the faithfulness of its portrayal of the man and the moment, his "Crossing of the Delaware" immortalized the birth of Liberty as a hard-earned fact, not merely as an ideal penned courageously in the Declaration of Independence.

This significant event is memorialized by many historical and educational features at Washington Crossing Park, Bucks County, Pennsylvania. These are supervised by the Washington Crossing Park Commission and the Department of Forests and Waters of the Commonwealth of Pennsylvania. We are deeply indebted to its present secretary, Maurice K. Goddard, for his guidance and ever helpful interest.

Many other individuals and groups have worked together to make history come to life at Washington Crossing Park—the Wildflower Preserve Committee, the Thompson-Neely House Committee of the Bucks County Federation of Women's Clubs, the Bucks County Chapter of the Daughters of the

American Revolution, the Bird Banding Station, the Bucks County Historical Society, the Patriotic Order of Sons of America, the American Legion, the Washington Crossing Methodist Church and its minister, the Reverend Thomas B. Everist, and many civic and patriotic organizations.

But for more than a century the single most effective memorialization of the historical event has been Emanuel Leutze's immortal painting. May the truth about it and its patriotic creator provide a bright and inspiring page of history for our young citizens. In today's troubled times, the painting's message of patriotism can carry the American cause for freedom not only across the Delaware but also across this great land to all the freedom-loving nations of the world.

ANN HAWKES HUTTON

Bristol, Pennsylvania

Acknowledgments

The author is indebted to several collateral descendants of Emanuel Leutze for the many old family letters that provided the mainspring for this book: Mrs. Charles Bowden, Mrs. William Price Webb, and Mrs. Louis Arnholt; also to two direct descendants, Emanuel Leutze's granddaughter, Marion Alice Leutze Rowcliff (Mrs. Gilbert J.) and his grandson, Rear Admiral Trevor William Leutze (USN Ret.).

She also wishes to thank the officers and trustees of The Metropolitan Museum of Art, James J. Rorimer, Director; Dudley T. Easby, Jr., Secretary; Mrs. H. D. Allen, Associate Curator; Albert T. Gardner, former archivist and present Associate Curator of the American Wing; and Murray Pease, Conservator of the Department of Conservation; for co-operation in making museum archives available.

The author also deeply appreciates the use of facilities of the Historical Society of Pennsylvania, the New York Public Library, and the Free Library of Philadelphia, with especial thanks to the latter's exceptionally helpful librarian, Caroline Lewis Lovett; the E. Lee Trinkle Library of Mary Washington College of the University of Virginia, and the encouraging interests of its Reference Librarian, Marguerite L. Carder, and Librarian, Dr. Carrol H. Quenzell.

Her gratitude is extended to Henry J. Dubester, Chief, General References and Bibliography Division of the Library of Congress, Washington, D. C.; Lucile U. Haseman, Reference Librarian in its Fine Arts Department; Henri Dorra and Horace L. Hotchkiss, Jr., of the Corcoran Gallery of Art in Washington; and Professor Vernon D. Tate and Isaac W. Windsor, Reference Librarian, of the Library of the United States Naval Academy, Annapolis, Maryland.

Invaluable help was also provided by Emil Metzger of Bristol, Pennsylvania; Dr. Hans M. Sylvester of Philadelphia;

Sonia D. Meurer of Emerson, New Jersey; and Thomas E. R. Smith of Harrisburg, Pennsylvania, who translated articles and many letters written in old German script.

The author also wishes to acknowledge her appreciation to Ruth R. Schmid for her valued secretarial assistance.

Credit should also be given for the quotation from Louis Pasteur, used as the title of Chapter 4, and for the quotation from Rudyard Kipling's poem, "If," reprinted in Chapter 6.

Finally the author extends her thanks to Henry T. MacNeill, widely known for his historical sketches, and Lloyd Eastwood-Seibold, versatile curator of the famed museum at Valley Forge, for the excellent illustrations included in the book.

ANN HAWKES HUTTON

Contents

Preface vii
Acknowledgments ix
1. The Early Years 1
2. Widening Horizons 15
3. Education in Europe 27
4. "Chance Favors the Prepared Mind" 39
5. Washington's "Unconquerable Firmness" 55
6. "If You Can Keep Your Head . . ." 69
7. Desperate Hour of History 87
8. Climax of a Career 105
9. The Successful Years 118
10. An End and a Beginning 133
11. The Painting Everyone Knows 145
Epilogue: The Painting Comes to the Delaware 161
Bibliography 178
Index 182

Chapter 1

The Early Years

An eager young man rushed excitedly out the front door of a small row house near the Delaware waterfront in Philadelphia. Suddenly he swung around and kissed his mother as she stood by the door. "Wish me good luck," he said and grinned, a warm, engaging grin, as he patted the thick portfolio under his arm.

That twenty-year-old youth was Emanuel Gottlieb Leutze (pronounced loit'-se), who was leaving home on January 17, 1837, to go on a long-planned trip to Washington with a portfolio of his paintings. He was optimistic, for he had been buoyed up by the praises of his Philadelphia friends and neighbors, as well as by some professional acclaim. Young Leutze's drawing master, John R. Smith, previously had urged him to enter his work in the Second Annual Exhibition sponsored by the Artists' Fund Society in Philadelphia.

The young artist had been proud to see a painting of his listed in the Society's catalogue, "No. 81—'Portrait of a Lady' —by E. G. Leutze—owned by the Reverend John Chambers." The exhibition had opened in late April of 1836, and had continued for two months in the rooms of the Society, at 194 Chestnut Street, Philadelphia. Leutze's canvas had won critical acclaim and consequently led to a promising opportunity. A publisher had engaged him to paint the heads of certain leading statesmen for engravings to be incorporated in a national publication. This exciting prospect entailed a trip to Washington and sittings by prominent political figures.

Leutze was well received at the Capitol. Senators and Representatives responded to the warmth and the exuberance of the tall, dynamic young man with red hair and bright blue eyes that twinkled with laughter and enthusiasm. But the outcome of the trip to Washington was inevitable. For one reason, the busy politicians, in a time of the sudden financial panic of 1837, could not give the time necessary for the sittings. For another, in that day when education in European art schools and an established reputation were prerequisites to securing the most prized art commissions, an unknown youth could scarcely expect success. Leutze left the United States Capitol—a disappointed and discouraged young man. As he walked sorrowfully from the building, he could not know that fourteen years later his work, "Washington Crossing the Delaware," would be exhibited in the same rotunda and be acclaimed enthusiastically on both sides of the Atlantic. He could not foresee that it would become the most popular work in America and be reproduced more widely than any other historical scene. Neither did he dream that eventually it would be owned by the Metropolitan Museum of Art where, in 1932, it stirred up a national controversy, from which it emerged victorious and again proved to be a chief attraction. On that particular occasion the painting was the overwhelming public favorite of the Washington Bicentennial Exhibition.

In 1952 the painting received gratifying national response when it was lent by the Metropolitan Museum of Art to the Washington Crossing Park Commission of Pennsylvania, for exhibition near the site that it depicts. That same year *Time* magazine reported, "Great paintings tend to come and go in the mind's eye, but for millions of Americans a first history book impression of 'Washington Crossing the Delaware' is apt to go on forever." The Metropolitan Museum of Art at that time labeled it "Perhaps our best-known and best-loved historical painting—long a primary attraction at the Museum."

One of the most surprising facts about America's best-known historical painting is the lack of information about its painter, Emanuel Gottlieb Leutze. The public seems to be interested only in the painting itself and the historical episode that it dramatized. This lack of interest in its creator partially explains the endless controversies about his nationality and his educational background.

Leutze's story is as dramatic and exciting as his famous canvas. It is the typical American story of the nineteenth century. Small European boy came to America, the land of his dreams. Here he lived, studied, and absorbed with deep interest the inspiring chapters of America's past. He dreamed about immortalizing those incidents on canvas and of becoming a great painter. After years of hardship and effort, he was acclaimed by his fellow Americans, who rewarded him by making him the most successful painter of his day. Here was an artist who could give the people a historical painting that they could understand, because he had such great admiration for the country of his father's choice and for its first leader, George Washington. Intense patriotism for America, the land of his adoption, characterized all his work.

As a nine-year-old boy, he had watched the sparkling water of the Delaware River as the ship he was on neared the port of Philadelphia. Then suddenly he spied the outlines of the then largest city in the New World. From a distance, the buildings and the church steeples reminded him of the toys he had placed under his Christmas tree the year before in Württemberg, Germany. But now he was in a great city in the United States of America, where he was going to live!

Emanuel Gottlieb Leutze was born on May 24, 1816, in Gmünd, Württemberg. That village, thirty-one miles northeast of Stuttgart, was famed then, as now, as one of the early centers of silver craftsmanship. Like many fellow countrymen of the period, his father, Gottlieb, who was a skilled metal craftsman, brought his wife Catherine and their children to the United States to escape political oppression.

The Germany of the early nineteenth century, having been

completely humbled by Napoleon, was a frustrated and defeated country. In 1805, Frederick William III took up arms on the side of France in order to gain some Austrian possessions. For favors received, he was forced to join Napoleon in his campaigns against Austria, Prussia, and Russia. Sixteen thousand Württembergers were compelled to march to Russia, and only a few hundred lived to return to their homeland. The poverty-ridden citizens, farmers for the most part, felt only shame and disillusionment.

The American Revolution, followed by the French Revolution in 1789, had stirred up an interest in freedom in the hearts of men throughout Europe. The Germans were acutely aware that the day of the personal rule and the abuses of their princes should come to an end. There were urgent demands for constitutional governments in the tax-ridden states.

The older Leutze dreamed about the wonderful political and religious freedom in the young country across the Atlantic. He no doubt had heard also of its great leader, George Washington. Had not their own Frederick the Great made public comment on Washington's spectacular military feat in crossing the Delaware River, thus turning the tide of the American Revolution at Trenton?

Did Gottlieb Leutze tell his children stories about that famous general who had made history in the New World and had given new hope to the Old? History does not reveal that fact; all that is known is that in 1825 Gottlieb departed with his family for the nation that was "conceived in liberty."

The older Leutze was a man of considerable education for his time. He had married Christina Catherine Miller,[1] a widow, who had two sons, Jacob and Henry, by her first husband. She was the adopted daughter of Jacob Maier, a comb manufacturer. After her second marriage, Leutze, a skilled mechanic, carried on the family manufacturing business.

Records show that Catherine's son, Jacob, had emigrated to America as a young man and had settled in Philadelphia. His

[1]Occasionally written "Muller."

mother, naturally, was as anxious to see him as Jacob was to have the family join him in the New World. Gottlieb's long letters to his stepson, Jacob, written in 1824, reveal a deep concern about the "importance of such a step." The letters, written in old German script, contained detailed information on the family holdings. The comb-manufacturing machinery, together with Leutze's savings, amounted to approximately $10,000— a considerable fortune in 1824—and included the calculated sale price of the house in Gmünd. Delay in consummating the sale of the property caused a year's postponement of the move to America.

In May, Gottlieb received formal state permission to emigrate to this country. In the late summer of 1825, the family, consisting of the father, Gottlieb, his wife Catherine, Emanuel, and his sister Louisa, sailed for America. It is not known whether Henry, Catherine's other son, sailed with the family or had previously joined Jacob. The sloop *William Henry* arrived in Philadelphia in September, and held the following items listed for Gottlieb Leutze—"thirty-four chests and trunks, two barrels, one hogshead, twenty-five bags, nine beds, four bundles, four washing bowls, and seven kegs."

The Leutze family joined the earlier German-American colonists who had settled principally in Pennsylvania and Virginia. The records of service of the German-American colonists in the American Revolution are impressively free of disloyalty. Throughout the War for Independence, the one case of a disloyal German contrasts sharply with those of the understandably great number of English Tories. The robust patriotism of the German Lutheran group is best exemplified by the Reverend Heinrich M. Muhlenberg, patriarch of the Lutheran Church of America. He passed on his strong love of country to his son, John, who was born in Pennsylvania in 1746. John, who accepted his first pastorate in Woodstock, Virginia, became an intimate friend of Patrick Henry and George Washington. Both these famous men helped him to secure a commission as Colonel of the Eighth Virginia Regiment.

For generations the German Lutheran colonists liked to tell the story of Colonel Muhlenberg's valedictory sermon. Probably the Leutze family heard about it when they attended services at the Zion Lutheran Church at Fourth and Cherry Streets, which had been founded in 1766 by the elder Muhlenberg. John Muhlenberg's sermon delivered in January, 1776, in part said:

> The endangered fatherland, to which we owe wealth and blood, needs our arms—it calls its sons to drive off the oppressors. The Holy Scripture says, "There is a time for everything in this world." A time to talk, a time to be silent, a time to preach and to pray—but also a time to fight, and this time has come. Therefore, whoever loves freedom in his new fatherland, he may follow me!

With that he laid aside his clerical robe and buckled on his sword as the congregation sang Luther's hymn, "A Mighty Fortress Is Our God." Drums rolled, men in the congregation followed their pastor, and within an hour 162 men had enlisted in the Muhlenberg Brigade that later distinguished itself in the Battle of Brandywine and checked the advance of the British. That brigade also skillfully covered the retreat of the American troops in Germantown, on October 4, 1777. After the British surrendered at Yorktown, Washington wished to appoint John Muhlenberg as military commissioner in Virginia, but he declined and returned to Pennsylvania, where he was elected to Congress to serve his country in yet another capacity.

The story of John Muhlenberg is but one instance of the patriotic heritage of the German-American colonists whom the Leutze family joined when they landed at High (Market) Street wharf in Philadelphia. Young Emanuel's eyes must have widened at the excitement this glamorous city afforded, for it was so much larger than his native Gmünd. The wharf was an astonishingly busy place, with produce boats crossing from Camden, New Jersey, to Philadelphia, and ferry boats passing each other constantly on the Delaware. The boatmen's rollicking songs added to the excitement, as these vied with the shouts of the laborers on the wharf.

A bustling Ferry House stood at the northern corner of High Street and the river front. Another frame building, on the southwest corner, served as a fish and grocery store. As the Leutzes walked along High Street up the hill from the wharf, they passed the long fish market, and, behind this building, the Jersey fruit and vegetable stand. No less than five tailor shops on the south side of High Street between the river front and Front Street greeted their astonished eyes. Philadelphia was indeed a fashionable city!

A tempting aroma of coffee drifted toward the family as they passed the famed London Coffee House at Front and High Streets, the crossroads of America. Farther on could be seen the old Court House at the corner of Second and High, and the graceful steeple of historic Christ Church.

Young Leutze's association with the Delaware River was destined to last throughout his life and give the lie to those critics who, in their ignorance, continue to say that Leutze "never saw the Delaware River." He saw it many times; lived near it, in Philadelphia, and traveled extensively on it at various times throughout his life.

Leutze, Senior, seemed lost in the large city, however. The contract which he had made with a Philadelphia printer named Ritter apparently did not work out satisfactorily. History records that in 1830 the Leutzes lived at 215 North Second Street, where Gottlieb tried to make a living as a comb manufacturer. It was a prominent business, for in the hair styles of the period combs were standard feminine equipment. Many materials were used—horns and hoofs of cattle, tortoise shell, ivory, hardened India rubber and, to some extent, German silver.

Manufacturing was done on a small scale by individual craftsmen, and it involved tedious effort and meticulous manual labor. Most of the combs were made from an ordinary cattle horn split in two main sections, soaked in water and, when soft, heated over an open fire. Next came a pressing process by metal plates. The teeth were laboriously cut by a gauged handsaw, a procedure that required patience and craftsmanship. After cutting, the teeth had to be tapered on grindstones, and each tooth then required rounding and smoothing. The polishing process was done on wheels built of soft calico disks.

Gottlieb Leutze had been well trained in the intricate craft of fashioning ornamental combs with silver decorations. He was an expert silversmith, a trade identified throughout the centuries with the town of his birth. He especially enjoyed using the small ribbon saws and finishing the combs with hand carving, at which he was an expert. But Gottlieb suffered from an incurable disease and his wife could barely keep the meager business going.

In order to help support the family, Emanuel had to leave school. He wanted desperately to go to art school to learn more about the subject that had absorbed all his dreams and ambition. But there was no money for such a venture. He was able, however, to enjoy the fine art collection in The Pennsylvania Academy of the Fine Arts in Philadelphia, an institution established in 1805 and the first and most noted in the United States. Its history is the history of American art. It dates back to 1791 when Charles Willson Peale made attempts to organize a school of art in Philadelphia. Three years later, this effort culminated in the Columbianum, which held its first exhibition of paintings in Independence Hall in 1795. At the Academy young Leutze could study both the Peale and the Stuart works on Washington. He could also observe the works of other noted American painters, such as Washington Allston, Benjamin West, Thomas Sully, John Trumbull, Henry Inman, and Bass Otis. The Academy also displayed a permanent gallery of casts of classical sculpture that attracted wide interest. Leutze likewise had an opportunity to study the exhibits in The Franklin Institute on Seventh Street near Chestnut, and just three squares away, on the corner of Ninth and Sansom Streets, was located the Peale museum.

Young Leutze liked to study the faces he saw in a room or on the street. Later he would attempt to recreate them on paper, for eventually he wanted to paint portraits of all the prominent figures of the day, in Europe as well as America. He could picture himself, when he would be rich and famous, living in a fine home and owning an elegant coach and horses!

Dreaming was the only escape the boy had from a frightening reality. His father's illness became critical and he had to endure agonizing suffering for months. This meant not only extreme poverty for the Leutze family, but also hours of nursing by the boy, whose cheerfulness seemed to bring some comfort to the ailing father.

For Emanuel those depressing days at his father's bedside helped to develop in him a deep compassion for others, a quality that marked his personality throughout life. The hours spent thus gave him an opportunity to draw, so he sketched faces and scenes endlessly. His father, noting his absorption, realized that the boy's talent was real. Leutze, Senior, knew the satisfaction of working with his hands, but he also knew that his son might some day know the satisfaction of creative work labeled "art" and considered a profession of great honor. But, as he watched his son, he wondered whether the boy would make a good living. As he studied the youth's careful persistence and seemingly endless flow of imagination and energy, he felt that perhaps, after all, Emanuel was one artist who would not starve!

Young Leutze dreamed that he would paint famous scenes from American history, and he envisioned his works hanging in the new Capitol at Washington along with the other famous paintings. He knew that the great works of Colonel John Trumbull in the rotunda dramatized scenes in America's history—"Burgoyne's Surrender at Saratoga," "Cornwallis' Surrender at Yorktown," the "Signing of the Declaration of Independence," and "Washington's Resignation of His Sword to Congress at Annapolis."

It is possible that Emanuel may have wondered why there

was not a painting of one of the most exciting events in the Revolution—Washington crossing the Delaware. The way to dramatize the significance of this great moment, young Leutze dreamed, would be to paint a scene representing both the danger and the courage of the crossing, for that was the climax of the careful planning which resulted in the inevitable victory of the Americans at Trenton.

The boy was lost in his dream. One day he might paint this great scene, he thought. But it would have to be a very large canvas—the largest in the whole world. He would put it on exhibition in Philadelphia, and his friends and relatives would see it and be proud of him. Engravings of it would be made and sold to people all over the world. He would be rich and famous, and maybe one day his work would hang in the Capitol in Washington!

Before he could attempt any large-scale historical scenes, however, he knew he must learn how to bring faces to life, how to portray the details of clothing, the tilt of a waistcoat button or the fold of a cloak. Emanuel Leutze was a perfectionist. He would spend hours studying light at a certain time of day, the details of a drape, or the worn threads of a piece of rope. This kind of artistry was not for the impoverished painter. His mother and sisters needed money, so, although still a boy, he made desperate efforts to earn a living by taking whatever odd jobs he could find.

His drawings now began to show great improvement over his first crude efforts. He particularly enjoyed sketching the dogs he was forever befriending. With scarcely enough food for the family, Emanuel would hoard scraps for his beloved dogs. One animal, a bulldog, became the subject of the most successful sketch of his boyhood.

Anxious to learn how to work in oils, he determined to take the big step himself. At the age of fifteen he started working on an imaginative and colorful scene, but he was too impatient to wait until the colors dried before the final touches. To speed up the process he placed the canvas near the fire and walked away, speculating on the surprise his family would have when he triumphantly showed them his newest work. On his return he found his canvas burned and blistered. Although the painting was obscured, it was not totally obliterated. The fire, strangely enough, had produced the intriguing effect of aging. His family and his friends, hoping probably to allay his disappointment, pointed out some of the painting's promising features instead of criticizing him for his carelessness.

Little is known of the tragedy of the Leutze family in those years other than the significant change in Desilver's Philadelphia Directory. The 1830 listing of "Gottlieb Leutze—comb mfgr," read, in 1831, "Catherine Leutze, widow of Gottlieb Leutze, comb mfgr."

Catherine Leutze found some small comfort in the listing; but she also knew that, with her uncertain health, she could not successfully carry on the highly competitive and exacting craft. She could possibly sell the unused ends of the horns for buttons and trimmings, but such sales would mean only a meager income. She also had her daughter, Louisa, to think of, as well as her son, Emanuel, who was a dreamer, forever working on miniatures and making sketches for their neighbors who paid him with praise instead of money.

The boy had many ideas for historical scenes, which was natural, for he lived in the tradition-laden part of the most historic city in America. Around the corner from his home, at 239 Arch Street, was the home of Betsy Ross, who had made the first American flag from a sketch which General Washington had given to her. Just four squares away was Washington's presidential residence. Emanuel was fascinated by the stories of George Washington, for at that time, scarcely more than twenty-five years after Washington's death, the memory of the great man was still fresh.

One cannot help wondering whether young Leutze read any of the same books about Washington that had so impressed the boy Lincoln, a few years earlier. As a man, Lincoln said that he recalled "reading in my youth a small book, *The Life of Washington,* [by the Reverend M. L. Weems] and of his struggles none fixed itself on my mind so indelibly as the crossing of the Delaware preceding the Battle of Trenton."

Did Emanuel Leutze read that same biography? It is possible, for few books were published at the time, and American history consisted primarily of the story of George Washington and the American Revolution. In all books and in popular fancy the "Crossing of the Delaware" was considered the turning point in the American struggle for independence. That exciting event made a vivid impression on the youngster who was studying and writing the language of his new country with considerable success. He was growing up in an era when American history was still in the making, and who knows but that he dreamed of one day retelling that dramatic chapter on canvas in a way that would make it live for generations of Americans.

At the river end of Second Street was the house where the American patriot, Lydia Darragh, is supposed to have lived, and near-by was the spot where Franklin used a front-door key in his electricity experiment. At the corner of Third and Walnut Alexander Hamilton had lived, and a few squares to the west was the home of Commodore Barry, who succeeded John Paul Jones as head of the American Navy. Just six squares away was the office of Thomas Jefferson, and near-by, Independence Hall. Those historic sites were the boyhood playgrounds of Leutze. The author would like to remind those who criticize Leutze's use of the American flag as the symbol of the new nation in his painting, "Washington Crossing the Delaware," that Betsy Ross was still alive when the artist was twenty years old!

Leutze soon began to experiment with portraits, but his fees were small and uncertain. He had had an impressive scheme for doing a series of all the prominent political figures in America, as mentioned at the beginning of this chapter. No matter how bad the circumstances, however, Emanuel was always optimistic, and his mood reflected the good feeling of the times. All over the country there was a stirring of nationalism. The tone had been set by James Monroe, who had been re-elected to the Presidency in 1820 with a single dissenting electoral vote. Party strife seemed to have disappeared, and the era was marked by strong patriotism and an aura of good feeling. New states had been added to the Union—Louisiana, Indiana, Mississippi, Illinois, Alabama, Missouri, and Maine.

Throughout Leutze's early 'teens, exciting things happened. Europe had been brought closer to America, as the first all-steam crossing of the Atlantic was made by the Dutch steamer, *Curaçao,* in 1826.[2] Michael Faraday had developed the magical electric motor and generator, and Niepce was improving a primitive two-wheeled bicycle and also managing to secure the first camera image. The most exciting event of all to young Leutze was the establishment of the first railroad line in the United States, in 1829, which ran from Carbondale to Honesdale in Pennsylvania.

The unexpected seemed to be happening everywhere. Why not to Leutze? He had youth's abiding confidence that a real opportunity would soon come his way. It did, as a result of the successful entries in the Artists' Fund Society Exhibition of 1836, previously referred to. He had obtained commissions to do a number of portraits in Philadelphia and Churchtown, Pennsylvania, and, although his fees were small, his unmistakable talent had earned him an exciting opportunity. On January 18, 1837, he started out on his exciting project in the city which would eventually become his home, Washington, D. C.

To dispel his mother's worry because he was so far away, he wrote, "The distance is not great. I can see you in two days if anything should occur." His postscript to his sister was typically "twenty": "You may indulge yourself now and blow my Fame all over the city."

To his sister's comment on his "nonsensical" letters, Leutze

[2]First steamer to make crossing chiefly under steam—the American ship, *Savannah,* in 1819.

answered that he wrote nonsense because "it does not become men to write of their feelings as women do. Females can always pour out their troubles on paper. It becomes them as does perfume, but 'tis man's part to *act* and to *speak*." He then added, "Tell Mother that I shall not return to Philadelphia before I can return with my pockets filled . . . besides I must see the world."

Chapter 2

Widening Horizons

The year 1837 was one of poverty and panic in the United States. A wave of speculation had been sweeping the country since 1833. Expansion was reckless, and the situation was further precipitated by the failure of some large business houses in England, that had invested heavily in American securities. Two factors had sharply affected the value of the securities— poor crops in the West in 1835, and the issue of Jackson's Circular the following year. Public lands had to be paid for in "hard" money. With a real panic across the country, no one was in the mood for portrait "sittings," especially for an unknown artist who did not have the currently essential background—education in the famed art capitals of Europe. Nevertheless, Leutze's Washington project opened important doors to the young Philadelphian. He was able to attend the Washington's Birthday Ball, and on the following day wrote his sister: ". . . [White] House is splendidly furnished. I wish you were here to see it." Its formality must have brushed off a bit on the twenty-year-old painter, because in the same letter he was prompted to scold his sister because she was "not Lady enough to fold a letter. I assure you it is easier discovered in such trifles than anything else. Neatness above everything characterizes the Lady of Breeding." He reversed his viewpoint in relation to her choice of a husband. "You must not be so fastidious in regard to beaux. Marry first and love afterward," was his worldly advice.

In another letter he urged her to get married as he was "tired of writing to 'Misses.'" He added such personal items as "I am getting as corpulent as a Dutch Burgomaster. They're feeding me on hominy, which you know is a great dish here."

While in the capital, Leutze managed to do some works for "high prices—$50 a portrait." Momentary success made him ecstatic, and in gay mood he wrote to his sister Louisa on February 16th:

> Plenty of girls here, but there is one far, far away, "a world above them all" . . . Do you know where Agnew's store is in 2nd [Street] below Market [in Phila.]? You'll see a pretty young lassie there, Miss Hillem. Tell her how good I am. If you can't tell her how good I am, why tell her a lie. Anything, anything, only tell her I am good or she will quarrel with you. Go there and buy a trifle and ask her whether she knows me. Notice how she'll blush. Tell her you're my sister. She'll love you then! . . . How's Mother? I can't write German or I'd tell her I am doing first rate here. . . . I am in the utmost glow of spirits, as happy as a bird. If I could only fly as quick to Philadelphia and return. Give my love, No, I can't spare any of that . . . Don't forget to write to your affectionate, loving and constantly faithful brother forevermore and ten days after.
>
> Leutze

Eventually Emanuel moved southward, and in April wrote to his mother from Fredericksburg, Virginia:

> You will be startled to see I am farther south. I left Washington on April 18th. At Mrs. Dodson's [in Washington] I was so much confined and you know that it is death for me to keep my peace for a length of time. I am so wild, and now, after the restriction I feel like a colt set free.

Leutze's high hopes soon dwindled. Discouraged and without funds, he was soon beset by a loss of confidence. A chance meeting with one of Fredericksburg's most prominent citizens, John Minor, 4th, brought about a turning point in his career. Minor, a kindly man with a deep interest in the problems of young people, gave Leutze the sort of encouragement that helped to keep his pride alive, by securing some commissions for him. Leutze also found the courage to attempt a large canvas. It portrayed the Biblical characters, Hagar and her son, Ishmael, as they followed a dried watercourse in search of water to quench the boy's thirst. This painting was the first of many scenes Leutze later painted, dramatizing the hardships and struggles of the valiant.

In spite of his despondency, the young painter enjoyed Fredericksburg. This was a fascinating inland city on the Rappahannock River and had been an important postal station with steadily increasing trade. Gold, mined in upper Spotsylvania and lower Culpeper Counties, was brought to Fredericksburg in exchange for goods. Even in 1837, the city retained something of its gold-rush aspect. Its leading citizens, however, were part of an exclusive and highly cultivated circle.

It was inevitable that Leutze's charm, good looks, and talent made him a popular figure among the elite of this socially minded town. He had an ideal patron in forty-year-old John Minor. Minor, a graduate of St. John's College in Annapolis, Maryland, was a well-educated aristocrat, a cultured patron of the arts, who had tried careers both at sea and in the legal profession. With great wealth to indulge any hobby, he abandoned active law practice to concentrate on Virginia history. He wrote a number of items for the *Literary Messenger,* and it is he who is responsible for the immortal Uncle Remus stories. Br'er Fox and Br'er Rabbit first came to life in the charming folk stories that Minor, a bachelor, loved to tell to children.

On the Minor summer estate, "Topping Castle," and the town house, "Hazel Hill," John Minor entertained lavishly and with the distinctive and gracious hospitality that marked the Southern culture of the period. In Virginia the classical civilization of the old South had reached a high point of development. Wealthy plantation masters still managed to live magnificently and to entertain with a lavish hand. They had many hobbies, well-stocked wine cellars, and private race courses. Such a world proved to be a heady experience for the attractive and impressionable young artist. Leutze's letters home reflect his reactions. One written to his sister on his twenty-first birthday shows the broadening horizons of the young Philadelphian. It reads:

> I did not think to be so distant from you on my birthday, but necessity knows no law. Now I'm far from home, and, altho I have not everything I wish, still, I should be happy if I was certain that you were so, . . . I'm thankful for the length of time I have been away from home, for it has taught me how to appreciate the Love of my Relations which I scarcely knew before. . . .
> . . . I saw the account of the Riot at Pennsylvania Hall; . . . Were you not much scared? Tell me soon how Mother is, I wish I was there to see her . . . Louisa don't you think you could get me the notes of [several old German songs] . . . I should be glad to have them, you know I dabble a little in music myself at present . . . If I ever can do so Louisa I must bring you to Virginia. It's a glorious place—very aristocratic, tho' you would be amused at the originality of the Negroes. . . . The other day a Negro of Judge Carlten's, who lives opposite Fredericksburg, told me, speaking of a mill, and the distance of the Road [to it] in these words "when that other mill was *ours*, we called it a *right smart mile*."—So it is with everything the master owns. . . .
> . . . Farewell, and give love to all especially Mother and tho' distant still think of me as
>
> Your wild brother,
> Leutze

Leutze was philosophical about the widespread depression of 1837. "The money market," he wrote in one of his letters, "is in a deplorable state all over the country—people are not too anxious to have their portraits painted, still I have work and should not complain." He found satisfaction in the fact that Virginians "value artists very highly. . . . [I] received a puff of a very good nature in the morning's paper praising our works and . . . respectability of character and deportment."

Soon he became absorbed in the life of the important Virginia city, and was carried away by the throbbing patriotism which was still alive in the Fredericksburg of 1837. At the time of his residence there, the City's Revolutionary heroes were still fresh in the minds of its proud citizens. Fredericksburg was the city of many a famed American—the boyhood home of Washington and James Monroe; the adopted home of John Paul Jones, the great naval hero, and of his two close friends, General George Weedon and General Hugh Mercer, both of whom, like John Paul Jones, had been born in Scotland. It was Jones who, when asked if he was ready to surrender to the British, made the immortal reply, "I've just begun to fight." That was the "never-say-die" spirit of the city and of its three best-known Scotch-American citizens, Jones, Weedon and Mercer.

Hugh Mercer had gone to Fredericksburg at the suggestion of his friend, Weedon, who had arrived in this country at the age of twenty-one. Weedon, who had married Mercer's sister, became a colonel of the Third Virginia Regiment. He was one of that inner circle of officers present in the early discussions of the plans to cross the Delaware River, on Christmas, 1776. That swashbuckling Scotsman, who had a dash of Irish in his make-up and a vivid sense of humor, was compelled to take over a sad duty after the death of his brother-in-law, Hugh Mercer, who died a hero in the Battle of Princeton on January 3, 1777. He went to live in Mercer's home, "The Sentry Box," and became the legal guardian of the Mercer children.

There was no more genial host in all of Fredericksburg than George Weedon, who for years had been "Mine Host of Rising Sun Inn" and postmaster in the popular Fredericksburg Tavern. He became the first president of the Virginia branch of the Society of the Cincinnati, and was ever the fiercely patriotic veteran who never forgot the Battle of Trenton that turned the tide of the Revolutionary War. During Leutze's first year in Fredericksburg Weedon's nephew, Hugh Mercer, Junior, made the following statement:

My uncle and second father, General Weedon, said that the brilliant victories at Trenton and Princeton were won at the most gloomy period of the great struggle for our independence. It was the crisis of the war and turned the scale in favor of our bleeding country.

It is believed that Leutze must have listened with interest to the stories of the special celebration formerly held during each Christmas season in Fredericksburg in memory of the event known as "American Crisis No. 1." In 1837, Hugh Mercer, Junior, put down on paper an account of the annual affairs which had been held at "The Sentry Box," a day or so after Christmas. The event featured a great festival and jubilee dinner. All officers who had participated in the Crossing of the Delaware with Washington came from near and far. Young Mercer, a small child at the time of the first celebration, was always granted the privilege of sitting at the banquet table. Two young Negro servants, bearing wooden muskets and dressed in full military uniforms, were stationed at the door. One was called Corporal Killbuck, the other, Corporal Kildee. The guests sang ballads, drank punch, and each year shouted the verses which Weedon had written for the occasion.

On Christmas day in seventy-six
Our ragged troops with bayonets fixed
*   For Trenton marched away.*
The Delaware ice, the boats below
The lights obscured by hail and snow
*   But no signs of dismay.*

Our object was the Hessian band
That dare invade fair freedom's land
*   And quarter in that place.*
Great Washington he led us on,
With ensigns streaming with renown.
*   Which ne'er had known disgrace.*

In silent march we spent the night,
Each soldier panting for the fight,

Though quite benumbed with frost.
Greene, on the left, at six began.
The right was with brave Sullivan,
  Who in battle no time lost.

Their pickets stormed, the alarm was spread
That rebels risen from the dead
  Were marching into town.
Some scampered here, some scampered there
And some for action did prepare,
  But soon their arms laid down.

Twelve hundred servile miscreants,
With all their colors, guns and tents,
  Were trophies of the day.
The frolic o'er, the bright canteen
In centre, front and rear was seen
  Driving fatigue away.

And brothers of the cause let's sing
Our safe deliverance from a king
  Who strove to extend his sway.
And life, you know, is but a span
Let's touch the tankard while we can,
  In memory of that day.

Young Leutze naturally responded to the bubbling fervor of the patriotically minded citizens of Fredericksburg and became a part of its lively younger set. For the Young Men's Club of Fredericksburg he painted a portrait of John Minor, 4th, seated in his office, surrounded by his books and curios. This work was treasured by the group until it was lost when Federal troops in the Civil War occupied the building in 1862, and it has never been recovered. Another painting of Minor, recognized as one of Leutze's greatest portraits, is still in existence, however.

The fees for these works meant a great deal to the struggling artist. In a letter to his sister sent July 20, 1837, he reveals the financial pressures he was feeling:

I *must* not return to Philadelphia for some particular reason and one is, just at present, I could not collect sufficient money to go there. I have been paying off my old debts at Philadelphia. I sent $80 dollars there yesterday, and will now enclose $10 to you. I am very sorry that I can not spare *more* at present. . . . I can do much better here than at Philadelphia and assure Mother that if I could do well there or sufficient to pay my expenses, nothing would take me from home. I am very busy at present, and have not quite finished my miniature. . . . Give my love to Mother and console her with the idea, that I am now doing so well, that nothing . . . at Philadelphia can compare with it. . . . and believe me I shall always strive to prove myself your loving

Brother

E. G. Leutze

Still working at a furious pace in an effort to pay his debts, he gave some thought, nevertheless, to marriage as a possible solution to his financial problems. Leutze discussed this problem in a later letter to his sister, Louisa, written from Taylorsville, Virginia, on August 28th:

I assure you I cannot face [my creditors] again before I have sufficient to quiet them and now I have such excellent prospects to do so, perhaps you wonder why I should always be talking of my prospects, when I can show you so little proof of it, but believe me I am in much better situation than I ever was in my life—what pleases me most is that I am considered as a *Gentleman*, quite a distinction in Virginia, wherever I go and consequently enjoy myself very much. You want me to confide in you and inform of my *Love* affairs—loving time is over with me. My object now is to get a rich wife which I can too—there is a Lady here in the house now who I have reason to suppose I can get, she is worth about $6,000 and . . . owns several snug little farms, but she is not pretty and therefore I shall not try to get her— Why should I marry if I cannot get a rich girl, I won't have a girl who is not pretty or well educated, and a girl of that description can get a wealthy beau—it would be wrong to "link [her] fate forever with someone's like my own." . . . —give my Regards to

all my Friends and *love* to all my Relations. Bye the bye, when are you going to get married?—Don't put it off to wait for your
Brother
E. G. Leutze

Louisa did not "put it off" very long. Shortly after the New Year, 1838, she was married. Leutze eagerly planned a visit home in April of that year. He tried to prepare his family for the changes they would see in him after his absence of sixteen months. He wrote:

> I have grown very proud since I travelled, I must acknowledge and you will find a great change in me in every way. . . . My health is excellent and nothing would tempt me to live in a city again if my profession would allow me to continue in the country . . . I never was very strong but at present I am quite a match for most men, Virginia men I mean. They are so much stronger than our northern city beaux.

On his way north he filled several commissions for portraits in Baltimore and arrived in Philadelphia in time for the Fourth Annual Exhibition of the Artists' Fund Society. He wanted to exhibit one of his canvases which seemed to be attracting considerable interest at that time. It was entitled "Indian Contemplating the Setting Sun," and had been purchased by P. McCall. The exhibition would provide an opportunity to have the work viewed by many.

Among the exhibitors in its Fourth Annual Exhibition were Rembrandt Peale, Thomas Sully, Thomas Birch, George Schwartze, Trevor McClurg, and Charles K. Stelwagon. The last three artists were Leutze's close friends. He named his second son for Trevor McClurg and his grandson, Rear Admiral Trevor Leutze, carries on the name. Charles K. Stelwagon remained one of Leutze's dearest friends throughout his life. The artist's knack for making friends was surpassed only by his even more impressive ability to keep them in spite of his world travels and exceedingly active career.

One of his dearest and most helpful friends, Edward L. Carey, of Philadelphia, was a sponsor of the Artists' Society. A prominent patron of the arts, he became interested in the struggling young artist and secured several commissions for him. However, Leutze felt the pull of his beloved Virginia and decided to return there.

The summer of 1838 found Leutze again in Taylorsville and painting several portraits. He stayed at the home of Mrs. Taylor who was "so kind, just like a mother." The city boy Leutze was fascinated with country life.

> The farmers of Virginia belong to the first class. . . . Imagine all the pleasures of a country life with all the charm of refined manners, you may have some idea of the life I lead at present—the most pleasant imaginable, almost like at home, and I have a servant to wait on me!

Louisa's marriage no doubt influenced her brother's thinking, for he began to give serious consideration to matrimony. On July 12th he wrote to Louisa:

> If I ever marry it will be a Virginia Lady. They are so gentle, so modest and amiable not [like] the energetic northern ladies. Energy is a delightful quality in a man but in a woman it conflicts with that sweet confidence and trusting reliance which is such a charm in a woman. There is a sweet, beautiful creature living not far from here who I should be glad to make your sister if I could. You were so kind as to give me a brother I see not why I should not retaliate and give you a sister. Fredericksburg seems like my home. I will be sorry to leave it and want to return. I have met some warm friends here.

Throughout the fall of 1838 Leutze continued to paint in Taylorsville and at the same time he worried about the situation at home. By Christmas of 1838 Louisa had a baby daughter whom she named Julia Leutze (at her brother's suggestion) Gebell. Two days before Christmas Leutze was feeling homesick. He allowed his mood to spill from his pen as he begged for news:

> . . . even the most trivial things will make me more glad as they will form a base upon which fancy can build her palaces and hope trace her promise of the pleasures of meeting again. I want

you to particularly tell me of dear Mother for "til life's silver cord be broken would I of her fond love be told."

His mother was an ill and unhappy woman as 1838 drew to a close. Louisa's young husband had left her, and she was melancholy and depressed. Leutze sympathized with both his mother and his sister, but his greatest concern was for the little girl, Julia, who, he believed, might be affected by the gloomy atmosphere. He wrote a long letter to Louisa, which gives an insight into the character of the twenty-two-year-old artist.

> And about little Julia, I would tell you much. You are a mother and must be conscious of the holy trust nature has given to you in your child. Do, dear sister, do be very particular in every breath you breathe to her and let it be with some regard to her welfare. You must remember the permanency of first impressions. The virtues or the faults, the honor or the shame of your darling, depend on you. You will, I am certain, strive to neglect no opportunity to implant deeply into her unblemished heart the holy principles of morality, of virtue, of honor and religion. When I say religion I do not mean superstition or hypocrisy, but that high sense of duty which we owe to our fellow creatures and our God. Our lot has been one which must impress all of us with the high necessity of those virtues which alone can guide us thru a world full of troubles and thorns.

Both his mother and sister needed money, but Leutze could do little for them. His letter of August 24, 1840, reveals his persistent financial troubles, as well as the bold front he was still trying to put on for his mother's sake:

> I do not like to add to your troubles by telling you a long tale of mine, . . . I merely write to you, that you may not deem me negligent,—you know I came here, with the intention of paying some debts I contracted when I was sick here last—I paid away all my money and find that I have not sufficient, the Bills amount to much more than I anticipated. That would be nothing if only the creditors would be a little lenient, they think I have more and am not willing to pay. I have made some money here, more than sufficient for my expenses, but that is all paid away and

I now feel the want of money more than I ever did in my life, ... but tell no one of my misfortune, I will abide the worst and may heaven assist to get thro—I have no money now and do not know when I shall have some. Mr. Lane has not been able to sell any of my pictures at Philadelphia or I should not have been as I am now. I will write to him to make some arrangements that he may get some money for me. Tell no one of this but tell Mother I am very well, and send her many Kisses.

Good night—
yours sincerely
E. G. Leutze

Leutze returned to Philadelphia to try a commercial venture, an opportunity that grew out of his long-standing friendship with John Sartain, a prominent Philadelphia artist and engraver. Sartain had accepted an inviting offer from a large banknote engraving firm in New York and had recommended Leutze for his former job as a designer for the engraving firm of Underwood, Bald, Spencer and Hufty, in Philadelphia. Historical records do not reveal what happened, but it is not likely that Leutze, ever a restless soul, could long tolerate the confinement of an office job.

His career seemed to be at a dead end, so he gave grave consideration to the wise advice of his patrons, Minor and Carey, that he must have further study abroad. To be anyone in the art world of the 1830's, one had to study abroad in Munich, Rome or Düsseldorf. At that time the famed academy at Düsseldorf dominated the art world. It was the Paris of that day.

Leutze must go to Düsseldorf, so with his patrons' help and his family's good wishes, he sailed for the country he could scarcely remember. The Leutze who left America in January, 1841, was an American citizen sailing to "a strange country," as he later wrote to his mother from Germany. So he made his "crossing," still with his dream of another "Crossing" which he wanted to paint. He could not know that ten years would pass before this other dream, become a reality, would bring him home.

Chapter 3

Education in Europe

In January, 1841, after a trying voyage, Emanuel Leutze arrived in Amsterdam, Holland. There he studied painting briefly, before going on to Düsseldorf, Germany. In Düsseldorf he settled down to work on the first of an ambitious series of paintings on Columbus. He called the first "Columbus Before the High Council of Salamanca." The artist's days were full— he put in hours of work when the light was best. The rest of the day he spent studying German and history. In the evenings Leutze exhibited his talent for making friends. His nervous mannerisms and intense enthusiasm marked him as a young man of talent and energy, but a number of prominent Düsseldorf persons added the term "genius" to his character. Leutze's originality of style and bold self-confidence startled and delighted the local art critics. His height, his red hair, and his restless American manner made him stand out in any gathering. It was typical of Leutze's youth and personality that he did not rush to the famed Düsseldorf Art Academy for help. Instead, some of its most illustrious members went out of curiosity to meet the astonishingly tall American with a mind as quick as his gestures and with an impressive command of the painting craft.

In the spring of 1841 Leutze was enjoying his most successful exhibition to date. Back home in Philadelphia in the Seventh Annual Artists' Fund Society Exhibition held in its new hall at Chestnut Street above 10th Street, the twenty-five-year-old artist had more exhibits than any other painter. He had listed his residence as "Philadelphia," and certainly his thoughts and hopes were there throughout April and May. The titles of his works indicated the scope of his intellectual approach to painting. It is also interesting to note that, unlike many of the other works listed, only one of Leutze's canvases had not been sold. The following paintings by Leutze were printed in the 1841 catalogue:

TITLE	OWNER
"Portrait of a Gentleman"	Dr. Comstock
"Portrait of a Lady"	Dr. Comstock
"Scene from Guy Mannering" Chap. XIII, Vol. II	William Mason
"The Return"	John W. Field
"Portrait of a Girl"	H. M'Cormick
"Portrait of an Artist"	Dr. McMurtrie
"Portrait of a Gentleman"	Dr. McMurtrie
"View Near Harpers Ferry"	Jacob Snider, Jr.
"The Poet's Dream"	Edward L. Carey
"Landscape"	Edward L. Carey
"A Madonna"	For Sale
"The Angels Whisper"	J. B. Okie

Perhaps thy charmed spirit hears
Tho' low, strange music of the spheres
For aged people say
When sleeping infant smiles, a band
Of unseen angels o'er it stand
And sing the child a lay.

Those works of Leutze provoked wide enthusiasm in Philadelphia, and Mr. Carey was delighted to send the encouraging news of the artist's success to his protégé in Düsseldorf, who turned out to be a showman as well as an artist. Leutze dropped hints of his Philadelphia success to the right people, and soon he was urged to exhibit his latest work, "Columbus," at the Düsseldorf Art Club. For weeks after its first appearance, the art colony of Düsseldorf buzzed with comments on the new young academic, and his temperamental way of drawing. The Düsseldorf School of Painters had never before seen anything like young Leutze's style—it was so fresh, so freely composed, and so self-confident in its whole interpretation. Director Schadow of the Art Academy expressed great satisfaction with the work and requested Leutze to offer it to the Art Union at Düsseldorf. Leutze did so and, to his delight, it was purchased.

The artist's success and the result of his first six months in Germany show in his letter dated August 2, 1841, written from Düsseldorf to his sister Louisa:

> Finally, after a long period of almost eight months I received a letter from Philadelphia. You can imagine how pleasant that was for me. . . . You must know that it is not due to a lack of feeling that I am not with you in Philadelphia at this time but I feel that things will change for the better not only for you but also for myself. For, a long time ago, I promised myself that I would not enter into any obligations without knowing that you and our dear mother are taken care of financially. You must know it pains me greatly that I cannot do anything at the present and that if it had not been for the purpose of helping you I would not have had the courage *to go to a strange country with little money and no friends.* [The italics are the author's.] But my firm belief in my industriousness will make me succeed. . . .
>
> I can relate much happy news about my circumstances here, and I am so much the happier that I have achieved my goal so early. Instead of having to spend my time in Germany as a scholar I have already won a position as a master craftsman. Believe me, I can hardly give words to my joy in order to share it with you.
>
> I have painted a picture—just think—which won such acclaim here—here at the greatest painting academy in Europe—that I was able to sell it immediately for 400 Reichsthaler—much higher than I was ever paid for a picture in America. And it was not sold to a private person but to a public society for the propagation of the arts! And the picture is in a field [historical scenes] in which I never before had an opportunity to work.

When I arrived here, I was happy to be immediately admitted by the best society and soon was showered with evidences of friendship. I feel that I am becoming very proud . . . suddenly to have conquered the years I expected to spend in Germany as a student, and . . . when I did not know how I would make a living. So I have already achieved my goal and, once having won a name in Europe as an artist, I need have no fear in America. Now just a short time of patience and the years of trial are past. My innermost wishes and hopes would never have placed me in the position which I have attained now and soon, very soon, a new dawn will open for us. In the meantime I hope that Lane paid the money still owing [apparently from the sale of Leutze's pictures] and that you need worry about it no longer. Whatever I can do, I will.

Give our dear mother my love. . . . Have patience only a little while longer and hope for the best.

I have not yet traveled farther, in spite of wanting to see our relatives in Württemberg but I had neither the time or the money to do so. But I hope to see them soon. . . . We live very comfortably here together with our American friends, the Schwartze brothers—I and my friend who traveled with me. But the weather here is very bad. Otherwise I have adopted the characteristics of a German artist. Can you picture me in a long painter's robe with a pipe reaching to the floor, a little cap on my head, long hair and a mustache? That is yours truly, the German Scholar and Artist!

Please give my best regards also to our brothers and consider all my letters sent to America equally directed to all of you. . . . I shall probably remain here for a longer period since I can put the finishing touches on my education as an artist. . . . Write to me very soon again about home. I remain your ever loving brother,

Leutze

That letter reveals much of Leutze's circumstances—that he was homesick for his family, and still plagued by finances, and still a foreigner in a strange country. He described his affectations with humor and found the picture of himself as "a German artist and scholar" amusing—further proof, if it is needed, that he was in fact, as well as mind, always an American. That letter also points out the incorrectness of those critics who have erroneously labeled him "that German painter."

Leutze was charmed by the beauty of the quaint German city of Düsseldorf. In that place the Rhine was as close to him as his beloved Delaware had been in Philadelphia. By 1830 Düsseldorf had become the nucleus of German romanticism. As an art center, it had been growing in importance ever since 1826 when Schadow, a talented artist himself, was appointed head of the Academy. Under Schadow, the fame of the Düsseldorf school made it the most popular European art academy of the 1830's and '40's. To dismiss the Düsseldorfian technique as "romantic," "baroque," and "superficial" is to repeat the definition of some modern critics who have not looked fully into the school's background. Basically, what was available to Leutze in the Academy was the graphic training of the engraver, a training the young artist had already mastered in America. What he did receive at the Academy, in addition, was some influence from the brilliant backgrounds and talents of his masters. Actually there were two, the Director of the Academy, Friedrich Wilhelm Schadow, and Leutze's master, Karl Friedrich Lessing, who had offered to give him lessons.

Lessing was a vigorous, truth-seeking painter, of whom the art critic, J. Beavington Atkinson, wrote in the *Art Journal* of September, 1865:

> . . . . He [gives to his works] their preëminent reality and . . . endows them with strong appeal and brings them close . . . to the spirit of the age . . . Lessing's pictures are . . . real as life and . . . manly as the grand historic characters they seek to honor.

That contemporary critic might easily have been writing about Lessing's pupil, Leutze, and his most famous painting, "Washington Crossing the Delaware," for that famed canvas is as "manly as the grand historic characters" it portrays.

Schadow was successful in building up a self-sustaining

community of artists at the Düsseldorf Art Academy. The school emphasized the value of well-rounded culture—the theater, literature, and philosophy, as well as art. Theatrical performances were frequently presented and historical events were reënacted. Music was important, and Mendelssohn was, for a while, one of the community.

The young men who studied art at Düsseldorf could not fail to feel the impact of German philosophy, for they had a wealth of intellectual giants to stimulate their thinking, such as Goethe, Schiller, Kant, and Schopenhauer. Young Leutze lived within the contemporary period of the influence of those great philosophers and poets.

At the Academy, the students spent their days painting and their evenings in reading and discussions of romantic poetry. Literature and drama were important parts of the Academy curriculum. The school reflected the forvor of its masters, Schadow and Lessing. It reached its height in 1851, but from that time on it drifted farther away from reality and deeper into sentimentality.

Although Leutze was surrounded by German culture and bright-eyed German girls, he talked, dreamed, and painted scenes dramatizing the past of his own country, America.

One of his letters included a nostalgic reference to the girl he had left behind in Philadelphia. Her name was Margret. A letter to his sister reveals his feelings.

> If I only had known Margret's feelings toward me earlier, I would have been certainly very much happier in Philadelphia. I will never forget when she said good-by to me. . . . Give my regards to all and please kiss Margret for me (that is if she will accept it) and also ask her to accept the book as a souvenir from me. I shall feel greatly honored if she does. Please write me about her as much as you know. I cannot say how much I shall enjoy . . . to hear from her, any time.

In November, 1841, although he had been away almost a year, Leutze was still homesick. He wrote:

> I can find none of the promised pleasure which is supposed to attend traveling, for the difficulty of hearing from friends and the constant anxiety and fear embitters every moment here. I feel this to be but a weary exile until I shall reach home again . . . It will be late spring before I can go to Württemberg as money is scarce and *I must waste no time.*

Emanuel Leutze was a young man in a hurry; he wanted to learn everything Düsseldorf had to offer him and then proceed to Italy for further study before returning to America. Accustomed to the freedom of his life as a working painter in the United States, the Academy seemed "like a prison" to him. He was not doing enough painting to satisfy his intense ambition; he felt he had to be a success quickly. However, for a short time, he worked conscientiously under the master, Lessing, on historical paintings. Actually, Leutze's genius as an artist made more of an impression on the Academy than the Academy did on the independent and gifted American.

Leutze's interest in the historical field reflected the trend of the times. In America the Romantic Movement had not been so active a force in art as it had in Europe, for there were no knights or monks or princes imprisoned in towers to depict! In Europe, art reflected the unhappy times—war and dissatisfaction with the present world. Historical scenes were an ideal escape; and they offered, as the critic, Muther, states, "What constitutes the prime condition of all art—that its contents must be some fact vivid in consciousness."

The artist, Delaroche, had skimmed the cream of historical scenes, so later artists had to dig for the unknown and the hitherto undramatized. Leutze found his first inspiration for historical works in the life of Columbus, who became his first hero, as typified in Leutze's first canvas of "Columbus Before the High Council of Salamanca."

Leutze's impressions of his Düsseldorf experiences are preserved in these words:

> For a beginner in the arts, Düsseldorf is probably one of the very best schools now in existence, and had educated an uncom-

mon number of distinguished men. The brotherly feeling which exists among the artists is quite cheering, and only disturbed by their speculative dissensions. Two parties divide the school—the one actuated by a Catholic tendency, at the head of which stands the Director of the Academy [Schadow]; and the other by an essentially Protestant spirit, of which Lessing is the chief representative. The consistency and severity . . . of the art taught at this school, . . . soon confirmed me in the conviction that a thorough poetical treatment of a picture required that the anecdote should not be so much the subject, as the means of conveying some one clear idea, which is to be the inspiration of the picture. But the artist, as a poet, should first form the clear thought as the ground work and then adopt or create some anecdote from history or life, since painting can be but partially narrative, and is essentially a contemplated art.

The best illustration of Leutze's view of his profession is found in his works, which, instead of portraying a mere scene or incident, have a moral significance—conveying some great idea such as chivalry, loyalty to truth, or patriotism.

Leutze worked tirelessly to complete the companion picture to his first Columbus canvas. This he entitled "Columbus in Chains," which he finished before setting out for Munich—the next stop on his grueling training schedule. That second work won a gold medal at an art exhibition in Brussels, and was later purchased by the Art Union in New York.

This painting, also known both as "The Return of Columbus in Chains" and "The Third Return of Columbus in Chains from Cadiz," continued to have an interesting history. In 1843 it was offered as a prize in the Annual Drawing of the Apollo Association—an organization in the United States formed by a group of persons interested in Fine Arts. Dues were used to purchase paintings from promising artists and each year a drawing was held and the work presented as a prize. In 1843 the winner was Richard James Arnold of Providence and Newport, Rhode Island, and Savannah, Georgia. Mr. Arnold's daughter had married a Talbot of Providence, and the painting was handed down in the family and now is in the living room of the interesting old Talbot House at Twenty-fourth and Delancey Streets in Philadelphia.

That particular painting was used as the design for a United States postage stamp in 1893. As a two-dollar stamp, it is one of the Columbian Series highly prized by collectors today. The search for the original painting began on Long Island and continued into Georgia. F. L. Lewton of the Smithsonian Institution took up the trail and eventually the painting was discovered in the mid-1930's at the Talbot residence in Philadelphia. The Smithsonian had been anxious to check the original painting because the stamp showed an extra figure on each side of the scene. It is not definitely known whether the figures were cut off the original Leutze work, but it is hardly likely that that had been done since the Alexander H. Ritchie engraving is identical with the original.

F. Ellis, writing for the weekly *Magazine of Philately*, September 17, 1938, stated that an engraver for the American Bank Note Company added the figures to fill in the stamp design. If so, it is the only known time when any engraver of a stamp changed the design of an original painting.

By the spring of 1842 Leutze had made all his plans to leave for Munich. Something happened that made it exceedingly difficult for him to leave Düsseldorf! He had met Julia Lottner, the beautiful young daughter of a distinguished colonel of the Rhenish Prussian Army. Julia was a sixteen-year-old beauty with level brows above large gray eyes and wore her long brown hair swept back from her brow. Leutze was fascinated by the Grecian quality of her beauty and wrote to his mother about his hopes to marry Julia as soon as he returned from his studies in Europe.

However, that spring a love-struck Leutze left Düsseldorf for Munich. There he studied under the famed painters, Cornelius and Kaulbach, and saw, in their superb style, the power of Munich as an art capital. After 1860, that city succeeded Düsseldorf as the leading European art center and continued to hold its leadership until Paris gained the favored position.

In Munich Leutze used every moment of his stay to advantage. He found time to complete his "Columbus Before the Queen," before proceeding to Italy. On the way there he stopped in Gmünd to visit relatives and family friends whom he could scarcely remember and saw the house in which he was born and the hill where all the Leutze children used to sled. He felt it would have been pleasant to linger, but he was anxious to see the feudal remains of the Hohenstaufen Castle. He spent months in that area, enchanted by its wildly dramatic scenery and intriguing legends. Leutze gained local fame by climbing one of the mountain peaks in a single day with no guide. He returned to its base exhausted and disheveled but, in typical Leutze fashion, he had done what he set out to do, and in a hurry as always.

In the Hohenstaufen country, he painted "Columbus' Return from America," "Sir Walter Raleigh's Farewell to His Wife," and "Cromwell at His Daughter's Deathbed."

While Leutze was studying and painting in Europe, he was also exhibiting in Philadelphia. His canvases in the Artists' Fund Society exhibits in 1843 and '44 indicate the scope of his work.

TITLE	OWNER
"Edwin and Elgira"	P. McCall
"Shylock—The Signing of the Bond Episode in the Merchant of Venice"	J. R. Ingersoll
"The First Music Lesson"	G. W. Snyder
"Cromwell Remonstrated with by His Daughter"	John Towne
"Prince Val, Vindicating Himself Before His Father"	Joseph Sill
"Scene from Shakespeare's Henry IV, Part II, Prince and the King"	

Leutze was as thorough a European tourist as he was a painter, for he visited almost every city between Düsseldorf and Italy. From the Tyrol he continued to Venice, the revered center of southern classical art, the goal of every artist of any age, the place that John Minor had urged him to visit.

Leutze arrived in Venice in 1842 and stayed in Italy for three years before returning to Germany. He was especially interested in the technical skills of the Venetians, who had learned to use oils in such an ingenious way that they could create a wonderfully accurate illusion of substances such as wood or cloth and of the variation in effects of light. The work of Veronese, who painted monumental compositions, fascinated Leutze. His "Wedding at Cana," one of the largest canvases in the world, teemed with colors and crowds. The Venetian school had tremendous influence on Leutze and on such masters as Rubens and Delacroix. Artistic and poetic minds have always responded to the charm of this old city. Leutze wanted to study Titian, Veronese, and the famous Bellinis, and to "warm myself in the sunshine of their colors."

He first saw a Raphael at Bologna, and felt an indefinable joy as he stood before the painting, "St. Cecilia." "But my joy was much impaired," he wrote, "by three or four scaffolds and easels with miserable daubs that were to be sent into the world as copies. I soon learned, however, by afterexperience, that scarcely any beautiful picture can be seen in Italy except through the fretwork of half a dozen easels."

Strong individualist that he was, Leutze did not share the enthusiasms of the average tourist. If he were not in sympathy with the subject of a painting, he was not able to overlook the content, no matter how brilliant the execution. Leutze was an "all-the-way" kind of person. In Raphael he saw an unforgettably beautiful reflection of the past, and in Michelangelo, a powerful and individual prophet of the future.

From Venice, he traveled to Rome, where he studied the famous masters, spending hours in museums copying their works. He made careful studies of Michelangelo and Titian and was fascinated by Titian's ability to stir the viewer's senses by color. He studied the naturalism of Caravaggio who avoided a too-perfect idealization of beauty by painting wrinkled skins and knotted muscles, a lesson Leutze never forgot.

Chapter 4

"Chance Favors the Prepared Mind"

In Rome, Leutze settled down in a small studio to do serious painting. One of his closest friends there was Daniel Huntington, who later became the president of the National Academy of Design and one of the leading figures in American art. Huntington has left observations on the "very careful and elaborate studies" made by Leutze in preparation for each canvas.

A fellow artist described him as he worked for hours on a picture. Leutze kept perpetually in motion, deftly juggling palette, cigar, and maulstick from hand to hand. He worked rapidly, completely absorbed and intent. Suddenly his repressed energy would seem to burst out of control, and he would break off from his work and burst into a rousing song or romp wildly with his huge dog, whose barking delighted him. Leutze engaged in frolics as vigorously as in work. He had noisy rows with friends and neighbors, none of which the participants ever took seriously. He loved excitement; his temperament seemed more Latin than American or Teutonic. He was unconventional in ideas as well as attire, and had an unbridled enthusiasm that matched his restless energy.

It was during his stay in Rome that Leutze painted "King Ferdinand taking the Chains from Columbus" and the "First Landing of Norsemen in America." This latter work, which won immediate critical acclaim and fame throughout Europe, gave Leutze an insight into the type of controversies which would inevitably arise with any publicized painting.

The painting had been commissioned by his Philadelphia friend and patron, Edward L. Carey. In 1844, Carey's private gallery was the finest in Philadelphia, and, for certain examples of American art, the best in the country. The philanthropist had merely submitted the title to Leutze and told him to handle it as he wished. Leutze proceeded to make his usual careful preparations before he began work on the canvas. He studied archeological specimens and fragments so that he could paint with historical accuracy. Not a detail of this picture was overlooked—the helmets, the mail, the curious Norse girdles of the men—all were studiously copied.

This work, "First Landing of the Norsemen in America," illustrates the accuracy of his exhaustive research. One of the figures in the scene is a small boy who, after the wearisome sea journey, shows joy and wonder as he clutches at grapes growing above his head. Lay critics, and perhaps a few jealous artists, questioned the presence of grapes in the scene and claimed it was an impossible botanical fact. Leutze, never one to weaken in battle, produced the page and line in the record of the Norsemen's landing, where the fact of their gathering grapes is recorded among the wonders of the new country. The proof silenced his critics for the time being.

The grape touch was favorably commented upon by one of the leading contemporary art critics, Henry T. Tuckerman, who devoted considerable study to this work of Leutze. He comments on the "rushing ardor" of the Norsemen "and the pose of the leader [as] extravagant and melodramatic. Some faults of execution are evident. Yet the whole is conceived in fine spirit. It is not a quieting picture. We must enter into Leutze's idea in order to enjoy it." The scene has excitement and reality. There is promise in the dilation of the bride's blue eyes as she presses her foot against her mariner husband's knee. Tuckerman continues, "Here is no flat and superficial attempt.

The man who did this was no shuffler; he was not afraid to call his soul his own; he had something decided to say with his color and drawing, and he has said it very emphatically. We are much obliged to him for speaking out like a man, instead of mumbling, and we feel at once that whatever may be his deficiencies in artistic skill, he has that primal and absolute claim upon our respect and affection which consists in *manhood*." No mumbler then or ever. Leutze would speak boldly from many a canvas!

The European fame of the Norsemen painting preceded it to America. Reports reached Philadelphia of the great interest taken in the canvas by leading European critics. The city swelled with excitement and pride because it would soon receive the already famed work of one of its own artists, Emanuel Leutze, who had reached a preëminence abroad "unparalleled since the days of Charles R. Leslie and Benjamin West."[1] Leutze shipped the painting from his studio in Rome, but before it arrived Carey died, and his friend, John Towne, purchased the four-by-six-foot painting from Leutze at the same price owed by Carey's estate.

Leutze had left Rome on May 22nd and traveled through Milan, Genoa, and Switzerland on his way back to Germany. He wrote a letter to his mother telling of his mixed emotions as he returned to Düsseldorf. He was saddened by the death of his old friend, of whom he said, "Carey was more than a friend. The remembrance of his goodness I will always carry in my heart. Through his efforts I can look forward to the future with pleasure. I intend to be married in October."

Leutze added that he returned to Germany "with great anticipation in my heart to see my beloved (Julia) again . . . I would like your approval and motherly blessing. I know, dear mother how much my fortune is in your heart. Pray it will be a success."

On his arrival at Düsseldorf, Leutze received a hero's wel-

[1] Dr. Horace Howard Furness of Philadelphia—Letter of January 1, 1904, to Robert D. Jenks, Esquire.

come. His gold medals and acclaim on both sides of the Atlantic made him a prominent figure in the social life of the city. He again became the current hero of the artists' colony —an enthusiastic young American with growing fame and fortune and a charm that swept both men and women along with his enthusiasm. It has been said of this artist that throughout his adult life, in either Europe or America, he was the center of a charming circle of friends and none was more charming than he. He had the warm friendliness of a child, the exuberance of an adolescent, but the cultivated mind of a keen student. In the highest social circles he was considered the most companionable and cordial of men. Small wonder that the young ladies of Düsseldorf considered him quite a catch!

Home and country were temporarily forgotten, for the famous young painter and Julia Lottner were married on December 16, 1845. Leutze was bound to Düsseldorf for a while longer.

From there he wrote to his mother and sister on February 26, 1846, explaining the reason for a longer stay in Düsseldorf:

> On the last steamboat I received two letters from you which made me very happy, since I had been expecting some for a long time. . . . But I learn with sadness that thou, dear mother, hast had the misfortune of losing the use of thy arm. It is a real comfort that Louisa will faithfully stand by to aid and care.
>
> You already know that I have been married since the 16th of December. I am sure that I need not write of my happiness, since you can easily imagine how it is. I live very comfortably a little outside the city. My wife is also very happy and becomes dearer to me every day . . .
>
> I am very happy that my picture was well received. I wish that I could always send something better . . .
>
> . . . I will arrange . . . that you can draw $25 every month in case of need . . .
>
> I remain as always
>
> Your
E. Leutze

Catherine Leutze had many worries while her son was in Germany. She was living at 507 North Third Street in Philadelphia, and trying to make a living by selling trimmings. Now this paralysis of the arm! At the time when she had been hoping for her son to return, he had married a German girl. She also understood that her daughter-in-law was highly born and a member of the best social circles in Düsseldorf. That probably meant that her parents would want her and her husband to stay in Germany, especially if there should be grandchildren. Would her son ever return to her?

Her granddaughter, Cornelia Bulkley Leutze, was born in the fall of 1846; and her first grandson, Eugene Henry Cozzens Leutze, the following year. The towering painter gazed in fascination at the tiny, red baby in the cradle. Little did he know at the time that all his hopes for his first-born son would be realized, and that Eugene would become a Rear Admiral in the United States Navy.

Another girl, Ida, arrived in 1849. Because the three small children and their adoring grandparents were in Germany, Leutze could scarcely expect to move his family to his own country. He had become in the middle '40's the "fair-haired" boy of the Düsseldorf Art Colony. His long study in Italy had crystallized his individual style and had, together with his dominant personality and independence of thought, made him question many of the rigid views of the Academy. He had established an atelier of his own, where eager art students sought his counsel and instruction. After all, Leutze was, at thirty-three, one of the most successful artists of the day.

He shared his studio with the most talented of the art students who went from America to study under him at Düsseldorf. One of those closest to him was Albert Bierstadt, who, although born in Düsseldorf, in 1830, had been taken to New Bedford, Massachusetts, as a baby and had been raised in America. When he was twenty-three, he returned to the great art capital for further study, and there he looked up his famed co-patriot, Leutze. Bierstadt and Leutze became firm friends.

They discussed their country and their respective plans to dramatize it on canvas. Leutze told Bierstadt of his ambition to do a series of historical works on the most dramatic moments in America's history and featuring the man most closely identified with those moments—George Washington.

Where Leutze was interested in bringing America's inspiring past to light, Bierstadt wanted to portray its present and its future. He was captivated by the wonders of the West and would talk for hours about the possibilities of its settlement, for there was exciting talk about unbelievable riches in mines throughout the new territories. Bierstadt, like Leutze, also studied under Karl Friedrich Lessing and Andreas Achenbach before going on to Rome. From there he returned home and traveled extensively in his beloved West. His Rocky Mountain landscapes—especially his works on Yellowstone and Yosemite—did for the West what the Hudson River School did for the Catskills.

One of the leading exponents of the Düsseldorf school was a young Ohioan, named Worthington Whittridge. He also sought out the popular Leutze as soon as he arrived at Düsseldorf in 1849. After five years' study there, he returned to this country and became famous for his Hudson River landscapes. While in Düsseldorf, he enjoyed sharing Leutze's studio, and so did another young American painter, Eastman Johnson. Johnson was a native of Lowell, Maine, the son of the Secretary of the State of Maine. Just as young Leutze had done before him, Johnson had gone to Washington to see whether he could secure any commissions by frequenting the committee rooms. Like Leutze, he was discouraged, and so the young painter saw the need for further study in Europe. He naturally headed for Düsseldorf.

Leutze was undoubtedly the best advertisement that art center ever had. As soon as Johnson arrived, he looked up Leutze, who graciously allowed the younger artist to share his studio for two years. Leutze's caricature of Johnson made at that time is recognized as a very clever and penetrating study.

Johnson also is rated highly by most modern American critics. Louisa Munson Bryant states in her *American Pictures and Their Painters:* "Johnson was big enough to study at Düsseldorf without losing his personality. His association with Leutze strengthened rather than weakened his artistic independence."

Leutze continued to execute a number of portraits. Sometimes he was paid for his work, but more frequently he was not. His historical scenes won success as fast as he could produce them. He continued his Columbus series with "Festive Reception of Columbus on His First Return from America," and also engaged in painting scenes of historical interest in both England and America, such as "Henry VIII and Anne Boleyn in the Park," "English Iconoclast," "Torquemada Persuading King Ferdinand to Dismiss Embassy of the Jews," "Puritan Surprising His Daughter Before a Madonna," "Storming of the Teocalli," and "Charles I Signing Strafford's Death Warrant." Whatever Leutze did seemed to turn out an instantaneous success. He drove himself at a furious pace, and as well as completing his canvases, he continued to work on preliminary sketches for his Washington works.

Leutze loved life and lived it to the fullest. He enjoyed several roles at the same time—successful artist, husband of a socially prominent woman, and adoring father of three children. Not only did he have a family to support in Düsseldorf, he also had his mother and sister in Philadelphia. He never forgot those two, who enjoyed both the fame and the financial rewards of their adored son and brother. But in spite of his work pace, he managed to continue his omnivorous reading. He had never forgotten his dream of having his work exhibited in the Capitol of his beloved America, and he studied constantly to learn authentic backgrounds for his proposed historical works. He planned to make Washington the central figure in all the scenes he had in mind, which meant that he had to know Washington the man as well as Washington the general. To do this he had to be familiar with those events which not only had molded Washington but also were, in turn, shaped by the strength of his character. Since Leutze was skilled in portrait work, it would have been a simple matter to have made a formal portrait of Washington. Already those by Trumbull, Peale, and Stuart had achieved lasting popularity, but the fame of Washington warranted other major efforts, and certainly Leutze's reputation would insure a certain degree of success.

Leutze, a man of great physical energy, a kind of Hemingway with brush instead of pen, no doubt found many of the Washington portraits to be, to him, pallid portrayals of a vigorous man. It is doubtful whether any mortal has ever enforced more rigid self-discipline than the sorely tried Commander in Chief. This meant an inevitable masking of emotions. In addition, Washington also possessed a natural reserve and shyness; he was a man of character and action, not of words. His leadership was based not so much on his exceptional intellect as on his unusual strength of character.

Prior to Leutze's time, no painter had successfully managed to portray Washington's active leadership in the American Revolution. The artist who would try had to have, first of all, a knowledge of Washington's role in American history and a real understanding and admiration for the national hero. Leutze, however, from the days when his youthful imagination was stirred in Philadelphia and Fredericksburg, to his vigorous and imaginative adult response to the "Father of His Country," was just the man to make the gigantic effort.

For several years before he started the first canvas of "Washington Crossing the Delaware," he made preliminary sketches of the principal figures. Inevitably he lavished the most attention on Washington's face and figure. The first President was, of course, the most famous American. In order to recreate Washington's features Leutze had to study the works of other artists and sculptors who had already portrayed him.

In Washington's time there were no photographers, but there were painters who hounded him throughout the greater part of his life. So annoyed was he at their persistence that he wrote in 1785, "I am so hackneyed to the touches of the Painter's pencil that I am now altogether at their beck and sit like Patience on a monument whilst they are delineating the lines of my face."

It is doubtful whether any other man ever had his features so frequently immortalized on canvas. Apart from his importance as the Commander in Chief of the first American Army and as first President of the United States, Washington was an ideal model, for he had heroic features and a majestic carriage. His manner and dress are legendary, so he should have been the answer to a painter's dream, but this was not the case. He disliked "sitting" for a portrait intensely, but eventually submitted to it as a duty. In this connection he once said, "What habit and custom can effect! At first I was as impatient at the request [to pose] as a restive colt. The next time I submitted very reluctantly but with less flouncing; now no dray horse moves more readily to the Thill [wagon shaft] than I do to the Painter's Chair."

Washington seemed to enjoy sitting for his genial artist friend, Charles Willson Peale. Peale had an intimate knowledge of public affairs and was suave enough to persuade Washington to relax. Usually, the very fact that Washington was posing made his face expressionless. Apparently, the only way an artist could get any life into it was by discussing either war or horses, both favorite subjects with General Washington.

Peale's son, Rembrandt, was also a painter, and executed the famous portrait of Washington standing beside his white charger. Another son, James Peale, also did several Washington portraits.

Charles Willson Peale was himself an interesting personality, a soldier under Washington in summer and a first-rank painter in winter. He was, like Leonardo da Vinci, a man of many talents. He stuffed birds, made harnesses, clocks, and even teeth, and it was he who made the dentures that gave Washington such a grim jaw line.

Gilbert Stuart, another famous painter of the period, was better known for his technique than was the military Peale, but the sophisticated Stuart was not so popular with General Washington. It is an interesting fact that when the Stuart head (called by Washington's stepson, George Washington Parke Custis, "the best likeness") was completed, Martha Washington refused to accept it, maintaining that it looked unfinished. Stuart preferred to keep it anyway, since he could sell a hundred or more replicas of the portrait at one hundred dollars each. The original painting was not sold until after Stuart's death.

Stuart maintained a studio at Fifth and Chestnut Streets in Philadelphia, but later decided it was too crowded there, so he moved to his stable in Germantown, then outside the city limits, where he painted three likenesses of Washington. The first portrait dissatisfied him so much that he destroyed it; the second is in England; the third one, "The Atheneum Portrait," which has been so widely copied, the artist kept. Two of the present Washington portraits in the White House are by Stuart. [The third is by Luis Cadena.]

Stuart's admiration for Washington became almost a passion with him. He expressed himself about the General's features in these words:

> There were features in Washington's face totally different from what I have observed in any other human being. The sockets of his eyes, for instance, were larger than I ever met with before and the upper part of the nose was broader. All his features were indicative of strong passion yet, like Socrates, his judgement and great superior command made him appear a man of different class in the eyes of the world.

Washington's eyes were, history records, a light gray-blue, but George Washington Parke Custis quoted Stuart as saying that he "made them deeper than they were in fact so that, after a hundred years have passed, they would be faded to the right color."

Another painter who portrayed Washington was an old soldier, the General's aide-de-camp, who was the son of the patriotic Connecticut governor, Jonathan Trumbull. Custis referred to Trumbull as the most successful portrayer of Washington's figure.

The market for Washington paintings became so popular that he was frequently painted by artists who had never even seen him. After seeing one of those works, Washington wrote: "Mr. Campbell, whom I never saw to my knowledge, has made a very formidable figure of the Commander in Chief, giving him a sufficient portion of terror in his countenance."

Portrait painting was a competitive business in Washington's day. A few grew wealthy at it; many at least made a living out of their work, because nearly everyone, from the poorest merchant to the most outstanding statesman, wanted not only to have his own portrait done but also those of his wife and children. Naturally there was great rivalry between the prominent artists who sought to paint Washington.

The keenest feeling of competition existed between Gilbert Stuart and the two Peales. To George Washington and to the Peales, Stuart seemed to flaunt his English background too ostentatiously. However, they recognized his ability, even though they could not warm to his personality. Stuart's wit and barbed tongue are undeniable facts. There is a story that in 1795, when Washington was sixty-three, both artists were making portraits of him at the same time. Washington, trying to get the paintings completed as quickly as possible, gave permission to Peale's son, Rembrandt, as well as his two other artist sons, Raphaelle and Titian, also to work on his portrait. He thought that he had the situation satisfactorily arranged when he gave the Peales three sittings of three hours each, and had Stuart work on alternate days. One day, while all the Peales were at work, Gilbert Stuart arrived unexpectedly. Finding four Peales in the room, he gave them all a condescending nod and soon departed. Later he told Martha Washington, "He is being 'peeled' all around. He is beset, madam, by no less than four of them at once. One aims at his eyes, one at his nose, another is busy with his hair. His mouth is attacked by a fourth."

It is generally agreed that, of all Washington's painters, Stuart was the most successful in portraying the face of Washington. When Leutze began his works on Washington, he studied Stuart's works so carefully that his paintings in the manner of Stuart are perfect likenesses of the original. In the Fine Arts and Literature Room of the Free Library of Philadelphia there is a portrait of Washington that most visitors assume is a Stuart one. The author had been under the same impression for years until the librarian of that department, Caroline Lewis Lovett, informed her that the work had been executed not by Stuart, but by Emanuel Leutze.

Leutze, always the perfectionist, was not even satisfied to use the most successful painting of Washington's face as a model; he preferred to study an accurate three-dimensional head of Washington, a bust by the French sculptor, Jean Antoine Houdon. Born in 1741, Houdon had, by the 1780's, become the most famed sculptor in the world.

The Houdon bust is generally accepted as the world's best likeness of Washington. The left side, especially, is supposed to be the most perfect and exact likeness of Washington in existence. A mask from this bust is what Leutze used as his model for the head of the Commander in Chief.

Leutze treasured this mask above all his other possessions, and even carried it with him wherever he went. It was handed down in its original case to his son, Admiral Eugene Leutze, who kept it for years, eventually giving it to the son of his father's great friend, Charles K. Stelwagon. Mr. Stelwagon later presented the mask to the Corcoran Gallery of Art.

The story of the making of the Houdon bust is very interesting. Congress had voted to erect an equestrian statue of Washington, but failed to follow up. Virginia then voted one thousand guineas for the statue, and commissioned Benjamin Franklin and Thomas Jefferson, who were then in Paris, to make the necessary arrangements with the great French sculptor, Houdon. Houdon refused to use the Peale portrait for a pattern and decided that a personal visit to General Washington was preferable. Franklin and Jefferson felt the sum offered by Virginia not large enough, but Houdon accepted the deal, with expenses added, and also a six-month life insurance policy.

The French sculptor left royal and wealthy patrons angry when he sailed for America in 1785. On October 2nd he reached Mount Vernon and remained there until the 17th, when he returned to Philadelphia to make further studies of Washington, before returning to France.[2]

Houdon spent the first week at Mount Vernon sketching the figure of Washington and working on the life mask. The process involved uncomfortable hours for Washington, because when his face was encased in the mask, he had to breathe through tubes inserted into each nostril through holes in the mask. The life mask did preserve the exact proportions of Washington's features, but it could not catch his personality and spirit. The stiff mixture used to make the mask was most uncomfortable and not conducive to a natural expression. It did take the impression of skin texture and of every blemish, the shape of his eyebrows and even slightly mussed hair along his hairline.

Houdon planned to use the mask for facial contour and proportions, but he was also anxious to catch and portray the power of Washington's personality. He next worked on a clay bust, spending hours trying to bring Washington out of the reserve into which he always retired whenever he was "sitting." The sculptor might never have succeeded except for the unexpected arrival of a horse trader, a brash fellow who ventured to impugn Washington's knowledge of values in horses. The horse trader's attacks made the face of the master of Mount Vernon light up in indignation. At once Houdon de-

---

[2] It took four years to complete the life-size statue of Washington. In Paris, Gouverneur Morris posed for the body of Washington. In 1796 the statue, now valued at several million dollars, was shipped to the capital at Richmond, Virginia, where it can be seen today.

lightedly caught the expression and immortalized it. The sculptor also used the life mask in molding a clay bust of Washington. The profile of that piece shows Washington's aggressive, far-seeing, dominant, and self-reliant qualities. However, the clay from which it was made has a weakness. Clay shrinks, after drying. Hence the proportions of the Houdon bust today differ by $\frac{1}{13}$ from the exact proportions of Washington's face in life. Furthermore, the clay, due to time and careless handling, became cracked, peeled, and broken, and consequently, in 1885, the bust had to be restored by another sculptor.

The Houdon life mask was a perfect likeness of Washington's features, but without expression. The clay bust showed a life-like expression interpreted by Houdon's genius, but of proportions smaller than Washington's own face. The likeness that combines the best features of both works is the mask preserved by Leutze, now in the Corcoran Gallery.[3]

Historical records state that either Houdon or one of his assistants cast one or perhaps two molds from the clay Houdon bust when it was still fresh and before it had shrunk perceptibly.[4] One of these is the Leutze-Stelwagon mask and it has preserved the combination of the exact features of the life mask and yet the forceful personality and spirited expression of Houdon's artistry in his clay bust.

Emanuel Leutze never saw George Washington, but he used for his painting the most exact and skillful portrayal of the famed American ever made. Leutze treasured this mask and had other masks and busts molded from it. He presented one to his good friend, John Briggs, the prominent Washington civic leader. In 1905 Mrs. Briggs presented it to the Mu-

[3]Eisan, Dr. Gustave A., and Conrow, Mulford S.: "The Leutze-Stelwagon Mask of Washington in the Corcoran Gallery of Art and Its Contributions," *Art and Archaeology*, Vol. 29, January–June, 1930.

[4]The well-known Clark Mills' reproduction of the Houdon bust was cast in 1853. This preserves the Houdon bust *after* it had shrunk $\frac{1}{13}$ its original size.

seum of the National Society, Daughters of the American Revolution. It is prominently and effectively displayed in the Society's Museum in Washington. It also has been reproduced in color for the cover of the Museum booklet.

One of the prized Leutze "heads" is in the possession of the Washington Crossing Park Commission and is exhibited in the new memorial building at Washington Crossing, Pennsylvania. In the auditorium is also exhibited the "Washington" Leutze painted from the mask, in his "Washington Crossing the Delaware."

This "head" was presented to the Park Commission by its former owner, the internationally known landscape artist, E. W. Redfield. When Mr. Redfield learned of the Commissioners' interest in the Washington head, through one of the commissioners, Donald DeLacey, he made the presentation. Mr. Redfield had been given the mask in 1926 by the Corcoran Gallery of Art in Washington. In this interesting way the real "model" for Leutze's Washington returned to Leutze's masterpiece, "Washington Crossing the Delaware," and the area which it depicts. This Leutze-Stelwagon bust was restored by the well-known sculptor, Harry Rosin, Instructor in Sculpture at the famed Pennsylvania Academy of the Fine Arts in Philadelphia. Mr. Rosin also presented the base for the exhibition of the bust. Of it he says, "This plaster cast of Washington's head is a cast from Houdon's sculpture."

TRENTON AND ENVIRONS

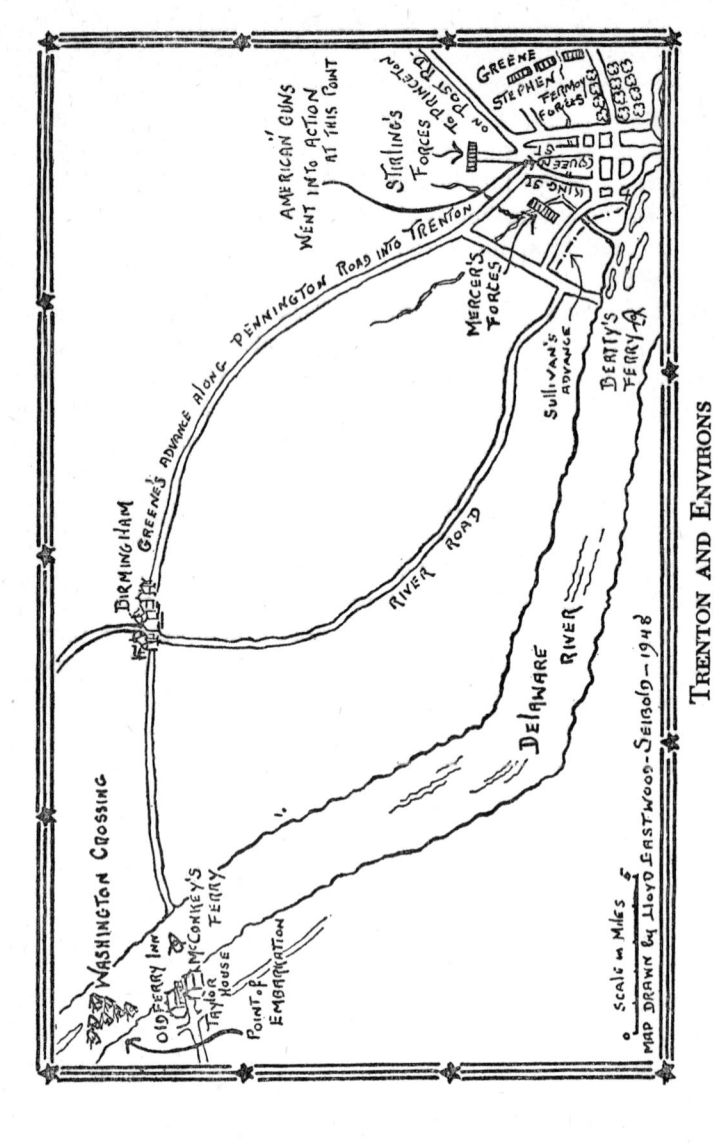

Including Washington Crossing—Showing Military Details Attending Washington's Surprise Attack, Christmas, 1776

Chapter 5

Washington's "Unconquerable Firmness"

Emanuel Leutze, with that instinctive sense of drama which characterizes all his works, chose the most critical event of the American Revolution as the backdrop for his "picture of Washington," his own name for the painting, "Washington Crossing the Delaware." The "Crossing" itself encompasses the most revealing decisions and definitive character study in the entire life of General Washington. The power of Washington's leadership is depicted at a time when "the spirits of the people were sunk to the lowest point of depression," according to Chief Justice John Marshall.

An insight into the unusual qualities of Washington's leadership is given by Marshall[1] who wrote, in *The Life of George Washington* (published for use in schools, 1838):

> Among the many valuable traits in the character of Washington was that unyielding firmness which supported him under these accumulated circumstances of depression. Undismayed by the dangers which surrounded him, he did not for an instant relax his exertions, nor omit anything which could retard the progress of the enemy. . . . To this unconquerable firmness—to this perfect self possession under the most desperate circumstances is America, in a great degree, indebted for her independence.

[1]Marshall was a lieutenant in the Third Virginia Regiment at the time of the "Crossing."

To appreciate fully why Leutze chose the scene of the Delaware River crossing for his Washington portrait, one must understand the events that led up to the heroic feat. The explanation for the tremendous significance of the "Crossing" lies in a full understanding of the trials that preceded it.

On July 4, 1776, while the Liberty Bell in Philadelphia was still proclaiming the new liberty, a British fleet was arriving in New York Bay. On July 12th, Admiral Lord Richard Howe, with about a hundred and fifty transports, had landed on Staten Island. Howe then joined his brother, General William Howe, who had disembarked ten thousand men there in late June.

Hessian troops, who had been hired for service against the colonists, about nine thousand in number, had also arrived on August 12th with their able commander, sixty-year-old Lieutenant General Baron Wilhelm von Knyphausen. Both British and Americans were preparing for the inevitable clash between the colonies and the mother country. Less than two weeks later, on the night of August 21st an exceptionally severe storm with strong winds, thunder and lightning swept in from sea over Long Island. The next morning the British troops landed. According to Henry Steele Commager and Richard B. Morris in *The Spirit of 'Seventy-Six:*

> The amphibious landing of the British forces on Long Island remains the most brilliant example of joint operations by the British in the entire war. Against the powerful British fleet, the defenders relied on land and island bases, but their artillery proved ineffective.

Opposing the twenty thousand invading troops, was Washington's untrained army of less than eight thousand men. General Nathanael Greene was ill, and General John Sullivan, blustering and unpredictable, was serving in his place. On August 24th, Washington, who was deeply concerned about Sullivan's uncertain abilities, placed Israel Putnam in command. The Indian fighter of the French and Indian War proved to be too old and too inexperienced, however, for this type of warfare. The Battle of Long Island, fought on August 27, 1776, with Putnam in command, was a disastrous defeat for the Americans. Six hundred men were killed and over one thousand were taken prisoners, among them General Stirling. Although Stirling's forces had stood with "great bravery and resolution," the green, unprepared Americans were simply outclassed, as well as outnumbered, by the better-trained, better-equipped British.

One unquestionably gallant stand in that battle was made by General Stirling and his men. Stirling had been ordered to an advanced position, with Sullivan at his rear. He kept his troops well in hand as he moved down the Gowanus Road on Long Island. Then, having been ordered to high ground, they gained the desired position. The enemy started to move in against Stirling, but he held his own against the right flank. Suddenly guns boomed from the rear. The enemy, unnoticed, had sneaked past the eastern end of the hills and were about to reach Gowanus Road and thus cut off Stirling's retreat to the fortifications at Brooklyn. The troops facing Stirling opened up with heavy artillery. With his retreat almost cut off, Stirling had only one alternative—to send his bewildered men through the marshes toward the Brooklyn line.

Marshall describes this event, in *The Life of George Washington:*

> Lord Stirling immediately directed the main body of his troops to retreat across the creek and, to secure this movement, determined to attack in person a British corps commanded by Lord Cornwallis. The attack was made with great spirit but, with the British General Grant advancing in the rear, his Lordship and the survivors were made prisoners of war. This attempt, though unsuccessful, enabled a great part of the detachment to cross the creek and save themselves in Brooklyn.

It was one of Stirling's battalions from Maryland, under Colonel William Smallwood, that performed the most dramatic and gallant action of the engagement. In order to hold off the enemy, so that the main body of troops might make an escape, the valiant group made a last defense at the front. Two hundred fifty-six of their six hundred eighty-four men were either killed, drowned or captured.

Stirling's connection with the unfortunate engagement on Long Island bears only the stamp of courage and duty. There were many mistakes among the others in command—General Sullivan was unfamiliar with the territory, and General Putnam made a sad guess of the enemy's intentions. This distraught man strode up and down the lines after the approach of the enemy and repeated over and over his famous command at Bunker Hill, "Don't fire, boys, until you can see the whites of their eyes."[2]

A British officer reported:

> A fellow they call Lord Stirling, one of their generals with two others, is prisoner, and a great many of their officers, men, artillery and stores. It was a glorious achievement . . . and will immortalize us and crush Rebel Colonies.

The British officer had reckoned without the guiding genius of Washington. That able strategist realized that the main body of his army, on the island of Brooklyn, could be separated from the New York contingent by the British fleet. General Howe made the fatal mistake of not following up his success by assaulting the Brooklyn fortification at once, a failure that gave Washington time to achieve a brilliant withdrawal.

Colonel Benjamin Tallmadge in his *Memoir* made the following report:

> On the night of the 29th of August General Washington commenced recrossing his troops from Brooklyn to New York. . . . To move so large a body of troops, with all their necessary appendages, across a river a full mile wide, with a rapid current, in the face of a victorious, well-disciplined army nearly three times as numerous as his own, and a fleet capable of stopping the navigation so that not one boat could have passed over, seemed to present most formidable obstacles. But in face of these difficulties, the Commander in Chief so arranged . . . that on the evening of the 29th by 10 o'clock, the troops began to retire from

[2]Freeman, Douglas Southall, *George Washington*, Vol. IV, p. 179.

the lines in such a manner that no chasm was made in the lines, but as one regiment left their station on guard, the remaining troops . . . filled up the vacancies, while General Washington took up his station at the ferry and superintended the embarkation of the troops.

As dawn approached, the men in the rear guard who were still in the trenches, became apprehensive. Several regiments were still on duty. Just as the sun began to rise, a providential fog began to appear and settle over both encampments. The last regiments had to wait at the Brooklyn Ferry for the boats to return from New York. When they had all been loaded and had shoved off, the astonished British troops appeared on the Brooklyn shore. They began firing from their muskets and field pieces into the fog, but by that time every American soldier was safe in New York. It was a magnificent action. Colonel John Glover's regiment of skillful fishermen from Marblehead, Massachusetts, did a remarkable job of ferrying the Continental Army across the foggy East River. We were to hear more of these stalwart sailors before the year 1776 was out.

Colonel Tallmadge concluded his memoirs on this retreat with the comment, "George Washington has never received the credit which was his due for this wise and most fortunate measure."

The experience on Long Island served as ideal training for another crossing, for offensive, instead of defensive, action and a crossing of the Delaware instead of the East River. Credit for the brilliant crossing of the Delaware to surprise the Hessians at Trenton, New Jersey, would be given to Washington by military strategists around the world, and by school children as well. The latter would learn about it from Emanuel Leutze's famous painting, "Washington Crossing the Delaware."

Lord Howe then decided to cross the East River and land his men at Kip's Bay [now 34th Street]. According to tradition, Howe, with his notorious weakness for wine and charming women, lingered for almost two hours at Mrs. Murray's[3]

[3] An intriguing portrait of Mrs. Murray was painted by Leutze.

residence on Murray Hill. Thus General Putnam and his thirty-five hundred men had an opportunity to escape to the American defenses on Harlem Heights, even though they had to sacrifice stores and artillery in so doing. At Harlem Heights the Third Virginia Regiment, commanded by Colonel George Weedon, already mentioned in Chapter 2, joined Washington on September 15.

The Commander in Chief was in great need of information about enemy fortifications, their number and different positions in New York and on Long Island. The task of obtaining it required intelligence, skill and bravery for it would be a most dangerous mission. A twenty-one-year-old officer, Nathan Hale, from Connecticut volunteered. He had been graduated from Yale, and General Washington, who was well acquainted with Hale's background, could count on the accuracy of his information. Nathan Hale had fulfilled his secret mission when he was captured and taken before General Howe. Hale frankly admitted his name, rank and his object in going within the British lines. Sir William Howe, without giving him the benefit of a trial, ordered the young soldier's execution the following morning.

As death approached, Captain Hale asked for a clergyman but his request was refused. He then asked for a Bible, and this request was also denied. As he waited for the execution, he asked for writing materials, which were given him, and wrote two letters, one to his mother and one to a brother officer. Captain William Hull of Connecticut wrote in his memoirs that Hale's dying words, which have become immortal, were, "I only regret that I have but one life to lose for my country."[4] It is said that Hale was hanged somewhere near the present site of Grand Central Station in New York.

Later an English officer, under a flag of truce, went to the American camp and informed Washington that Captain Hale

[4] Campbell, Mrs. Maria Hull: *Revolutionary Services and Civil Life of General William Hull; Prepared from His Manuscripts,* ... New York: 1848.

had been arrested within the British lines, condemned as a spy and executed that morning.

General Washington admired the young officers under his command, and accepted Hale's death with a heavy sense of responsibility and sorrow. He promptly dispatched an American flag to accompany Hale's body to its burial.[5]

Howe moved farther into New York and thus threatened Washington's main army. On October 18 Washington decided to retreat to White Plains, then a remote country site. Ten days later the Americans were confronted by Howe and Knyphausen the Hessian commander. The British advance was checked by Captain Alexander Hamilton's artillery, but eventually Howe won a hill position, but made the mistake of waiting for reinforcements before following up on the attack. Again Providence came to Washington's aid, and a storm further delayed Howe. Meanwhile, Washington was able to move his troops north, with his main forces still intact.

At that point, Howe made an abrupt change of plans and moved southward toward Fort Washington at the northern end of Manhattan. Washington did not know the reason for the move at the time. The reason was the action of an American traitor, William Demont, who had deserted and had turned over the plans of Fort Washington to the British.

Washington had already concluded that Fort Washington should be abandoned. He advised General Nathanael Greene to evacuate it, but left the decision to his subordinate. The bad judgment of the young Rhode Island general was costly—it resulted in the loss of twenty-nine hundred troops, ammunition, and provisions, and was one of the most crushing defeats of the Revolutionary War.

November 17th proved to be a red-letter day for the Hessians. They climbed the rocks to Fort Washington at the top

---

[5]Commager, Henry Steele and Morris, Richard B., *The Spirit of 'Seventy-Six*, p. 475. Such a reference would indicate the use of an American flag even *before* Christmas, 1776, and would substantiate Leutze's use of it in his painting.

of a hill overlooking the Hudson, and within two hours took the fort. The regiments of Colonels Johann Rall and Friederick von Lossberg formed two lines, and the Continental Army had to march between them, depositing all guns and stores as they filed through the lines. It was a humiliation the Americans did not avenge until the crossing of the Delaware and the Battle of Trenton more than a month later.

In his report to Congress, Washington said:

> The loss of such a number of officers and men, many of whom have been trained with more than common attention will, I fear, be severely felt. But when that of the arms and accoutrements is added, much more so, and must be a farther incentive to procure as considerable supply as possible for the new troops, as soon as it can be done.

The British proceeded to follow up on their victory with dispatch, and two nights later, under Lord Cornwallis, they crossed the Hudson. The next morning their artillery was set up on top of the Palisades. General Greene, having learned by experience, hurriedly evacuated Fort Lee. Along with much needed tents and blankets, the Americans left behind some of the letters of the brilliant journalist, Tom Paine, whom a British officer referred to as "that scoundrel Common Sense man."

After the abandonment of Fort Lee in November, Washington detached Stirling who had been exchanged as a prisoner of war, on October 7th, to watch coastal landings. The Commander in Chief had confidence that no sights or comments would escape the attention of this trained observer. Toward the end of November Stirling returned from the New Jersey coast to New Brunswick, New Jersey—or Brunswick as Washington called it—and awaited the arrival of Washington and his ragged army.

General Stirling was held in high trust by Washington and played a vital role throughout the American Revolution. His role was second only to that of Washington in the momentous "Crossing of the Delaware" Christmas, 1776.

In an army where loyalty varied as much as ability, where other officers, for one reason or another, might question the capabilities of their Commander in Chief, Stirling never once wavered in his devotion. He was, first of all—with the possible exception of General Hugh Mercer—Washington's oldest friend among his officers. American born, he was the son of James Alexander, who came to this country from Scotland. The elder Alexander distinguished himself as a colonial in many ways. He was made Surveyor General in New York and New Jersey, and also became famous for his legal knowledge.

It is in the field of law that James Alexander is best remembered by posterity. His brilliant defense of Peter Zenger represents the high point of his career. Zenger was jailed for libel because, in his New York *Journal*, he criticized the governor of the State. As a result of Alexander's efforts on behalf of Zenger, he was disbarred, but resumed practice the following year. Zenger was eventually acquitted in 1735, in the celebrated case that established freedom of the press. Although the case occurred forty years before the American Revolution, it has been called the "germ" of American freedom.

Alexander's lively, imaginative son, William, was nine years old at the time, and one day he would be known as Lord Stirling. No doubt he listened in fascination as his father expressed emphatic views on the importance of the rights of an individual to speak, to think and to print the truth as he sees it—for this man was a father for a boy to imitate and to remember.

William first saw military service in the French and Indian War. He became the aide-de-camp and private secretary to General William Shirley, the governor of Massachusetts. After General Edward Braddock, the English general, was killed at the Monongahela on July 9, 1755, General Shirley became acting Commander in Chief. Shirley subsequently had to return to England to explain the failure of the French and Indian War—a failure for which he was not to blame. He was justifiably disillusioned and unhappy, so it is not surprising that he urged his devoted young secretary, William Alexander, to accompany him. For Alexander, the trip promised to be an exciting event; furthermore, he felt that he could help to vindicate his Commander in Chief, whose conduct of the war had been unfairly criticized. Braddock, who was actually largely responsible for its failure, was dead. It was primarily Alexander's testimony before the House of Commons that secured justification for Shirley.

Young Alexander's charm of manner, his poise, and his logical mind, made a tremendous impression on the members of the English Parliament. He was wined and dined by the highest dignitaries in England—a heady experience for any young man. Several elderly men of distinguished lineage persuaded Alexander that he was the rightful heir to the estate of the Earl of Stirling; in fact they persuaded a jury that he was the male heir of Henry, fifth Earl. Later, when the House of Lords passed on the case, they ruled that Alexander had not fully established his descent. Alexander, on the basis of his own research, however, felt that the title was rightfully his. The principal gain to such a title would have been the acquisition of certain territorial rights of property in America that had been granted to William's ancestors. Convinced, as was the jury, that he had the right to this title, he determined to use it for the rest of his life, so from that time on he was known as Lord Stirling.

Back in America, it was natural that Lord Stirling opposed the Stamp Act. He soon followed principle with action, and six months before the Declaration of Independence was signed, he acted with typical vim and valor. With members of the regular army under his command, and a few of his neighbors from Elizabeth, New Jersey, he undertook a dangerous mission. Embarking on board a pilot boat and leading three smaller vessels, he proceeded out to sea at night under the nose of the *Asia* man-of-war and her tender, which lay at anchor in the Bay of New York, and attacked an armed British transport. The fact that he had only small arms, and that the transport was a ship of three hundred tons mounting six guns, intimidated him not at all. The only important fact was that the transport was carrying stores for the enemy at Boston. Lord Stirling captured the warship, and the following day conducted it into the port of Perth Amboy, New Jersey. Of this action, Congress, on January 29, 1776, declared: "Resolved that the alertness, activity and good conduct of Lord Stirling and . . . others who assisted . . . were laudatory and exemplary."

Stirling was a man who had the courage of his convictions, but costly convictions they proved to be. With his powerful friends in England, his large landed estates in New Jersey and New York, he would have been in a far more favorable position under English rule. As it was, his lands, which were sold in the devalued Continental money, meant enormous losses from which his estate never recovered.

Stirling was a distinguished person—handsome and with a great deal of personal charm. He was the genial and experienced general who anxiously awaited the arrival of Washington at Brunswick. Eventually it was he, more than any other officer, who encouraged Washington in his decision to switch the tactics of the American Army from defense to offense and, by the brilliant stroke of crossing the Delaware River on Christmas night, turn the tide of the American Revolution. The question remains, did Leutze include Stirling in his famous painting of "Washington Crossing the Delaware"? Since guessing who was in the boat has become a national pastime, the author suggests that anyone who is interested might compare the original portrait of Stirling by Bass Otis, in Independence Hall in Philadelphia, with that of the officer, hand raised to his tricorne, who is seated toward the stern of the boat in the Leutze painting. There is a striking similarity that cannot be ignored!

Before the Continental Army reached Brunswick, it had experienced several narrow escapes and was constantly pursued by the growing number of British troops. The losses of Fort Washington in New York and Fort Lee directly across the

Hudson River, had freed more British troops for field action in New Jersey. While the two forts had been in the colonists' hands, the British had felt the need of a strong New York garrison. With the fall of the forts, the British troops could be released from New York and join Howe's pursuit of the Americans across New Jersey.

Washington, who had lost about five thousand men during the previous three months, knew that he was too weak in manpower to attempt any entrenchment at the temporary headquarters in Hackensack. Retreat across the state was the only alternative, and it was not an inviting one, but with some three thousand men he miraculously managed to escape being trapped between the Hackensack and Passaic rivers.

On November 19th Washington wrote to his brother, John Augustus:

> It is impossible to . . . give you any idea of our situation, of my difficulties and of the constant perplexities . . . I meet with, derived from the unhappy policy of short enlistments . . . I am wearied almost to death with the retrograde motion of things and I solemnly protest that a pecuniary reward of twenty thousand pounds would not induce me to undergo what I do.

An extract from the letter of an English officer, written about this time, conveys the smug assurance of the British at this point of the war: "Lord Cornwallis is carrying all before him in the Jerseys . . . the rebels retreating most precipitately toward Philadelphia . . . In short, it is impossible but that peace must soon be the consequence of our success."

Washington reached Newark on November 22nd, and was joined there by his rear guard which had remained at Hackensack until the last possible moment, and had then burned the bridge behind them in "nick-of-time" fashion.

Defeat seldom depressed General Washington for any length of time. He was familiar with the topography of this country and counted heavily on this knowledge in his retreat. But, with desertions increasing hourly, he was becoming discouraged in his efforts to get reinforcements both from the state of New Jersey and from a slow and often unwise Congress.

In Newark, a patriotic Presbyterian pastor named Alexander MacWhorter joined the American Army. He was an able strategist whom Washington frequently included in his conferences. On November 28th, Washington abandoned Newark, just as the British entered the city. It is difficult to see how the Americans managed to survive and to conceal their weakness. For example, a very small detachment commanded by Colonel Elisha Sheldon of Connecticut, apparently was the only cavalry protecting the flanks from the impending British advance. Those men, middle-aged or older, were an unimpressive-looking group, who wore odd bits of clothing, and instead of carrying carbines and sabers, had only fowling pieces such as those used for shooting ducks!

When Washington reached Brunswick, he was faced with the loss of hundreds of men. The terms of enlistment of the Maryland and New Jersey militia expired December 1st, and the men demanded their discharges and, almost to a man, left for home. This action encouraged many more desertions, and it was not surprising that some of the Americans, insufficiently clothed and fed, joined forces with the well-fed, smartly uniformed British. The local farmers, who for the most part were Tory in sympathy, preferred dealing with the well-paying British. Enthusiasm for the cause of independence was as low as the spirits of the hungry American troops.

General Washington refused to be infected by the widespread gloom and continued to look ahead. From New Brunswick on December 1st, he wrote to Congress:

> I have sent forward Colonel Humpton to collect proper boats and craft at the ferry for transporting our troops, and it will be of infinite importance to have *every other craft,* besides what he takes for the above purpose, secured on the west side of the Delaware, otherwise they may fall into the enemy's hands and facilitate their views.

Washington also sent General Maxwell on this project, which proved to be one of the most significant in the whole Revolutionary War. His aides pointed out the costs and the scarcity of money available for food, but the Commander in Chief, with his usual foresight, knew that if he did not secure those boats immediately, there would be little need for food later!

Even at this gloomy stage, Washington had some offensive action in mind. On November 30th, from Brunswick, he wrote to General Charles Lee:

> The advantages they have gained over us in the past have made them so proud and sure of success that they are determined to go to Philadelphia this winter. I have positive information that this is a fact and because the term of service of the light troops of Jersey and Maryland are ended they anticipate the weakness of our army. Should they now really risk this undertaking, then there is a great probability that they will pay dearly for it for I shall continue to retreat before them so as to lull them into security.

Well aware that the enemy was only a two hours' march away, Washington made a semblance of preparation for resistance and deceiving the pickets in order to gain time. On Sunday afternoon, December 1st, a British column approached the Raritan bridge while others neared the stream where it was fordable. Again quick-thinking Washington ordered the bridge destroyed, and retired toward Princeton under cover of a brisk artillery fire from Captain Alexander Hamilton's batteries.

Though not yet twenty years old, Hamilton was an experienced fighter. He had fought in the Battle of Long Island and every engagement following. History paints an appealing picture of him—small and slender, marching beside his cannon, his cocked hat pulled down over his eyes. As his guns successfully covered the army's retirement, records state that he absentmindedly gave a congratulatory pat to his cannon as if it were a favorite horse.

Chapter 6

"If You Can Keep Your Head . . ."

Washington's army in the early winter of 1776 numbered barely three thousand. Many of his men were without shoes, stockings, and even shirts. Blankets and other supplies had to be left behind in the retreat because there were no wagons to carry such equipment. The men thought longingly of abandoned tents, as, during the early December nights, they lay huddled together on the bare ground. Lacking the proper cooking equipment, they used their ramrods in attempting to heat whatever rations were available.

Most of the soldiers in the field wore linen hunting shirts, which were filthy, ragged and often the sole covering of vermin-infested bodies. Dr. Benjamin Rush noted, with regret, the lack of woolen garments. Fevers, pneumonia and dysentery were rampant. Even the dreaded typhus appeared. The condition of the ill and wounded was, as General Greene described it, "beyond description and shocking to humanity." One surgeon's mate had to care for five battalions. Medical supplies had been exhausted for weeks. There were no bandages and the only drugs were the rudimentary ones sold at country apothecary shops—rhubarb, ipecacuanha, and Glauber's salts. Small wonder that few who fell survived.

General Washington fared little better than his men. He, too, as well as his secretary and aides, sometimes slept on the bare ground. His personal servant was, as Washington said, "indecently and almost shamefully naked."

These were, in truth, "the times that try men's souls." The Americans were no "summer soldiers." Of these men, Thomas Paine, never one to overpraise, wrote, "all their wishes were one, which was that the country would turn out and help them to drive the enemy back." Their suffering, the indifference of many Jersey colonists, and the significance of this period to the cause for freedom stirred Tom Paine to pen his immortal words in *The American Crisis*.

Paine, at the very height of his reputation as a patriot and writer, had shouldered a knapsack as a Pennsylvania militiaman. He was a valuable addition to the army, but his most effective weapon was a pen rather than a sword. Throughout the past year his *Common Sense* pamphlets had swept the colonies. In all the history of publishing, there has never been a more spontaneous sale. According to Henry Grady Weaver in his book, *The Mainspring of Human Progress*, "It has been estimated that out of a population of three million people, more than 300,000 bought copies of the book. Translated into present-day terms, that would correspond to a sale of around 14,000,000 copies."

In the flight from Fort Lee, Paine had lost his baggage and all his private papers, but he would never be without his pen! From Newark on and at every place the army stopped, he worked all night on the forceful words that were to help the troops through the first American Crisis.

In the light of history, it seems incredible that Washington's men escaped destruction for Cornwallis could almost certainly have defeated the Americans with ease. Confident that he could annihilate the fragment of the army he was pursuing, Cornwallis had sent a message to Howe for permission to attack before Washington could cross the Delaware. Howe's reply probably saved the American Army for he said he would join Cornwallis immediately. His "immediately" meant almost a week, and gave Washington the opportunity to reach Princeton on December 2nd, and from there lead his bedraggled army to the Delaware River.

Why had Howe allowed this lapse of time to give the hard-pressed Americans their one chance of escape? The only plausible military explanation was the necessity of getting proper supplies to his troops. But probably the best explanation is not military. The fact is, Howe was having a rollicking good time in New York. His constant companion was Mrs. Joshua Loring, a "flashing blonde" who shared Howe's fondness for gambling, and delighted in high stakes. Howe was happy in the present and supremely confident of the future of the war.

Before the entire American force had crossed the river to Pennsylvania on December 7th and 8th, Howe and the British vanguard marched into Trenton in hot pursuit. Tory-minded inhabitants urged him to hurry and to capture some of the Americans who had not yet been ferried across the Delaware. But the cautious Howe, fearing a trap, decided to halt with his army. With only a detachment of light infantry and a few Hessian riflemen, he proceeded to the Delaware River.

From the afternoon of December 7th through the early morning of December 8th, boats had been constantly carrying supplies and Washington's troops across the Delaware. The number of large Durham boats that American scouts had located, previously used to carry iron from upstream furnaces to Philadelphia, far exceeded the straggling army's needs. Townsfolk, who had gathered at the scene, laughed at the pitiful army and its determined leader, but it was the rebels who laughed a short time later as the British advance-guard, with colors flying and bands playing, marched grandly down to the banks of the Delaware. They could not find a single boat in which to pursue the Americans who greeted them with derisive fire from the western shore!

Cornwallis led some of his troops upriver, but they could obtain no boats for pursuit of the Americans. Howe also sent men down the river as far as Burlington. The answer was the same, "No boats to be found anywhere!"

When did Washington first decide upon the offensive of crossing the Delaware and making a surprise attack at Trenton? It was probably in his mind at Brunswick when he ordered all the boats along the Delaware to be gathered together. It was also hinted at in several of his letters to General Charles Lee. A superficial conclusion that the decision to cross on Christmas night was arrived at during a Christmas Eve conference at General Greene's headquarters in the Merrick House, near Washington Crossing, has occasionally been assumed by those who rely solely on a reference made by the historian, W. S. Stryker, in his *Battle of Trenton*. According to Douglas Southall Freeman, the definitive Washington biographer, this is a tradition not substantiated by documentary evidence.[1] Those who claim that the decision to cross was made on Christmas Eve ignore the realities both of the preparation necessary for the difficult operation and of communication problems in 1776. As Freeman has stated in his *George Washington,* "Details were worked some days prior to Christmas."[2]

There were many reasons for immediate American action. The citizens in Philadelphia were in a state of panic. Hysterical gossip about the arrival of the Hessians floated around every street corner. Congress was gravely concerned. One day it passed a resolution condemning as "false," rumors that it intended to abandon Philadelphia; the following day it asked General Washington to include this resolution in his orders to the troops. Washington, knowing Congress well, refused. On the very next day, Congress did exactly what it had resolved not to do—it fled to Baltimore!

On December 12th, Washington wrote to Governor Trumbull of Connecticut, "Nothing hinders the passage of the enemy but the want of boats which we have been lucky enough to secure." Washington was incurably modest; his se-

---

[1] Freeman, Douglas Southall, *George Washington,* Vol. IV, n. 306.
[2] *Ibid,* 308.

curing of the boats was certainly farsightedness rather than luck!

It was fortunate for the Americans that Howe overlooked or possibly disregarded having rafts built. Some forty-eight thousand feet of lumber were available in Trenton at that time, according to reliable estimates. Why Howe did not make use of the lumber for boats is just another baffling example of his seeming lack of energy and initiative. He was apparently loath to attempt to bring the war to a quick conclusion. It would be easier to wait until the river froze over and then he could cross with his men. Such a rumor was picked up by Washington's spies and passed on to the Commander in Chief. In several letters he commented on this possibility and linked it with a British attack on Philadelphia.

The excited citizens of this then-largest city in America were expecting the Hessians at any moment. As early as November 22nd, Samuel Chase had written to the Maryland Council of Safety, "It is reported General Howe meditates an attack on this city." David Rittenhouse, the first director of the United States Mint at Philadelphia, had said to the Freemen of the City, "Fellow-citizens, it is my duty to inform you that our enemies are advancing upon us and that the most vigorous measures alone can save the city from falling into their hands."

By mid-December business in Philadelphia had practically suspended. Frightened groups clustered in coffee houses and discussed the latest war news. Many troops, whose terms of enlistment were up, filed into the city instead of staying with their regiments where they were so badly needed.

On December 15th, Colonel John Cadwalader wrote to Robert Morris, the famous Revolutionary financier, from Bristol,

> For God's sake, why did you [the Congress] remove from Philadelphia? You have given an invitation to the enemy. You have discovered a timidity that encourages our enemy and dispirits our friends. The sky may fall or some lucky circumstance happen,

THOMPSON-NEELY HOUSE
Washington Crossing State Park, Pennsylvania

that may give a turn to our affairs ... I have run off with complaints, and am led to make them by the ... gloomy countenances seen everywhere I go except among soldiers.

Certainly the soldiers posted by each of the ferries on the Delaware and encamped close to the Thompson-Neely House, at what is now the Bowman's Hill area of Washington Crossing State Park, had reason for their gloomy countenances. They crawled into bushes and beneath rocks, making use of any available protection since they had no tents to shelter them. Their uniforms were ragged and their shoes—only the lucky ones still possessed them—were beyond repair. An orderly-sergeant in the regiment of artillery left his own account of the privations suffered by Washington's troops. Joseph White, a bombardier in Captain Richard Gridley's company, wrote, "The privation and suffering we endured is beyond description. No tent to cover us at night; exposed to rains night and day; no food of any kind but a little raw flour."

The fact that there were few volunteers is certainly understandable. From Bristol, Pennsylvania, on December 13th, John Bayard wrote to the Safety Council in Philadelphia:

> We are greatly distressed to find no more of the militia of our state joining General Washington at this time, for God's sake what shall we do, is the cause deserted ... and shall a few brave men offer their lives as sacrifice against triple their number without assistance?

From New England came Governor Trumbull's voice:

> Is America to be lost? Is she to fall victim to the rage of a lawless tyrant? God Almighty forbid! Our army to the westward —barefoot, fleeing the enemy! May God give us a spirit of wisdom, fortitude, and resolution in this evil day.

A few brave voices cried out, but many were silent—indifferent to the cause, or worse still, secretly plotting its defeat.

Europe, as well as most of America, had lost faith in any possibility of success. The French were not interested in helping a losing cause. Voltaire, the French philosopher, wrote: "Franklin's troops have been beaten by the King of England. Alas, revolution and liberty are ill-conceived in this world."

Greene wrote, "The tide of publick sentiment [is] at a stand and ready to run through different channels, the people refusing to supply the army." Adjutant General Joseph Reed wrote to Washington, "Something has to be done."

We know that, as early as November, 1776, Washington had an offensive plan in mind and hinted at it in a letter to Major General Horatio Gates:

> If we can draw our forces together, I trust under the smiles of Providence, we may yet effect an important stroke or at least prevent General Howe from executing his plans [to cross as soon as the river froze solidly and take Philadelphia].

On December 14th Washington found it necessary to call on his old friend and trusted officer, Lord Stirling, to ride to Morristown, New Jersey, to learn from General Charles Lee himself something about his intentions. The arrival of Lee's men was essential to Washington's plans. Lee was unpredictable, to say the least. He had been a former British army officer, and was both neurotic and egocentric. He had, however, achieved a military reputation that impressed a number of officers and politicians, and was not overlooked even by General Washington. An earlier message from Lee had been quite incoherent so it was necessary for someone to see him personally. That person had to be aware of both Washington's present situation and his plans for future action. Naturally, Washington chose Stirling, who was most impatient for offensive action.

That versatile officer had many qualifications for his important role as one of Washington's leading strategists in the plan to make a surprise attack at Trenton. As Surveyor General of New Jersey, a position formerly held by his father, Lord Stirling knew the state better than any other officer. He had a set of the best maps available, many of which he himself had drawn. An expert on logistics, he also enjoyed a considerable reputation as an astronomer. Fifty years old, Stirling was Washington's second oldest officer, yet he rode off to Morristown in spite of icy roads and an acute attack of rheumatism.

Stirling's ride on December 14th was one of the most important in the entire Revolutionary War. His orders were to learn the condition of the various forces, when the columns could be expected, etc. The letter of December 14, 1776, that he was to deliver to General Lee stated:

> Use every possible means, without regard to expense, to come with certainty at the enemy's strength, situation and movements; without this we wander in a wilderness of uncertainties and difficulties and no plan can be found upon a rational plan.[3]

That letter furnishes a strong clue to Stirling's important place in the crossing of the Delaware. Another clue is disclosed in Washington's reply to General Sullivan's message that General Lee had been captured. The letter read: "Stirling was fully possessed with my ideas when he left me, for the measures you and he may judge necessary to adopt."[3] Therefore, it is the theory that earlier conferences between Washington and Stirling must have taken place. Daily discussions among officers inevitably led to rumors and on December 18th, the reporter Christopher Marshall noted in his diary that reports of an operation against Trenton were circulating around Philadelphia.

Stirling's place in Washington's bold plan to attack the British at Trenton is indicated from another direction. The enemy's position on the Delaware almost demanded it. Washington pored over the maps of New York and New Jersey that had been prepared by Stirling as Surveyor General. As Stirling pointed out, General Howe had the road along the entire British side of the "nose" formed by the Delaware between

[3] Freeman, Douglas Southall, *George Washington,* Vol. VI, pp. 370–376.

Trenton, Bordentown, and Bristol. The British had supply lines from this river road to South Amboy and to Brunswick. If boats became available, or if the river froze, Howe could attack directly south from Trenton on the road to Philadelphia, or march around the nose, cross in the rear of the Americans, and take the city.

Stirling's surveys and maps were to play a large part in Washington's momentous decision. Stirling was the very one to take the same kind of daring initiative he had shown that January night more than a year before, when he had captured the British transport. Even his enemies anticipated such an action. Before the Christmas attack, General James Grant, who had temporarily replaced Lord Cornwallis, wrote to Colonel Johann Rall at Trenton:

> Washington has been informed that our troops have marched into winter quarters and has been told that we are weak at Trenton and Princeton, and Lord Stirling has expressed a wish to make an attack upon these two places. I don't believe he will attempt it, but be assured that my information is undoubtedly true, so I need not advise you to be upon your guard against an unexpected attack at Trenton.[4]

Grant had reason to be both contemptuous and apprehensive. Cornwallis, preparing to return to England, was sure there would be no further campaigns for the Americans, "even in the spring." Grant's contempt for the American Army had been justified by reliable British Intelligence reports; however, grudging admiration for the two American leaders, Lord Stirling and Washington, made him uneasy. Hence his Christmas Eve warning sent to Colonel Rall who was gaily celebrating in Trenton. Grant had remembered the determination displayed some twenty years earlier in the French and Indian War by the young Washington, then a Virginia major. Nor did he underestimate the valor and daring of Lord Stirling. Major General Stirling was put in charge of the river defense

[4] Stryker, William S., *The Battles of Princeton and Trenton*, p. 116.

ENTRY ROOM

Thompson-Neely House, Washington Crossing State Park, Pennsylvania; Furnished by Bucks County Federation of Women's Clubs

by the American camp four miles up the river from McKonkey's Ferry. Grant was well aware that Stirling was quartered at the Thompson-Neely House, located by the foot of Bowman's Hill, the best look-out along the Delaware River.

Colonel Rall was confident that a surprise attack by the Americans was not only remote but quite impossible. The rebels seemed about to disintegrate. General Charles Lee, of the dashing military reputation, had been captured by the British. The "five thousand good troops in spirits" of whom Lee had boasted to Washington on December 4th, turned out to be only two thousand men in poor condition when they arrived at the Delaware camp under General Sullivan on December 20th.

The pattern of failure that had begun on Long Island in August and continued throughout the fall with the retreats from White Plains, Fort Washington, and Fort Lee, seemed to be reaching its climax. The dissolution of the enfeebled army by the end of December appeared imminent. The conservative British publication, Dodsley's *Annual Register*, concluded its 1776 report on the American situation with the statement, "Everything seemed to promise a decisive event in favor of the royal arms, and a submission of some of the principal colonies was hourly expected."

Was there any hope for victory as this humiliating campaign neared its close? Hope lay in character and not campaign; it lay not in military maneuvers, but in the minds of the men who led them. Character is the key to the amazing success of Washington's crossing of the Delaware on Christmas night, 1776, and the resultant victory at Trenton.

Exemplifying John Marshall's statement, Washington "omitted nothing that would retard the progress of the enemy." So thoroughly was the task of collecting all available boats for the Americans performed, that later testimony about Howe's failure in the Jerseys revealed the fact that the British, on arriving at the Delaware River, had found only two boats on a mill pond!

That strategy had meant that Cornwallis and Howe were forced to abandon pursuit of the hard-pressed Americans at the very moment when they were least able to survive an attack. The boats had saved the American Army from its pursuers, but could they be used to ferry the freezing and starving rebels back across the Delaware for a surprise attack at Trenton? Or would the freezing weather make the river solid enough for the Hessians to cross on foot and attack the Americans?

By December 20th, Washington was fully convinced that the British planned to cross the Delaware after the first solid freeze and to take Philadelphia. He must therefore cross first —on Christmas night! Numerous conferences must have been held in order to arrive at that decision, but there is no documentary evidence of any.

As Douglas Southall Freeman points out, the Merrick House conference near Washington Crossing on December 24th makes an interesting anecdote, but no source is given for it. In view of the time of the crossing—Christmas, a Christmas Eve Council of War would inevitably become a neighborhood tradition. Conferences were undoubtedly held, in great secrecy, at several of the headquarters.

Robert Morris wrote to Washington on December 21st that he had been informed of the preparations to cross to the Jerseys. At the same time, Nathanael Greene hinted at plans "to give the enemy a stroke in a few days." Washington's own correspondence refers to the plan in a letter written on December 23rd to Colonel Samuel Griffin, expressing regret that Griffin was not going to Bristol, ". . . in order to have conducted matters there in cooperation with what I hinted to you as having in view here." Robert Morris's letter of December 26th to Congress stated, "This maneuver of the General had been determined on some days ago but he kept it as secret as the nature of the service would permit."

From these various references it seems safe to assume that the plan was discussed both in Washington's headquarters at the Keith house two miles inland from the Delaware River, and in Lord Stirling's headquarters at the Thompson-Neely House. Formal, written records of those conferences would scarcely have been kept because as Washington himself later remarked, "The success of the enterprise depended too much upon the secrecy of it, not to have used every precaution of concealment."

The story of one secret conference that is legendary, but so strengthened by tradition that it should be included in this book, is that of Washington with one of his ablest spies, John Honeyman, a trusted informant on the situation at Trenton.

Back in the discouraging days at Hackensack, New Jersey, that rough and ready Scotch-Irishman had offered his services to Washington. He had agreed to act as a Tory, and no one, even on Washington's staff, was aware of his association with the Commander in Chief. As a butcher, Honeyman dealt freely with the British in and around Trenton and was considered a British spy.

Tradition states that on the afternoon of December 24th, Honeyman walked out on the river road and managed to attract the attention of American scouts, who promptly arrested him and took him to General Washington. Washington asked all his officers to withdraw, and ordered the guards to shoot if Honeyman attempted to escape. After a half hour's conversation Honeyman was placed in prison and ordered to be courtmartialed in the morning. During the night, undoubtedly according to Washington's plan, he escaped, recrossed to Trenton, and told Colonel Rall the Hessian, of the episode, giving him a doleful account of the condition of the American army. The information reassured Rall, who had been hearing rumors about activity in the American camp.

Honeyman had also reported to Washington about the sudden change of attitude toward the British on the part of many of the prosperous, and until now Tory-minded, New Jersey farmers. The reason for this was the farce of the "protection papers" which were being issued by British officers. These promised pardon for anyone who had taken up arms and, in return for "Remaining in a peaceable Obedience to His Majesty and not taking up arms, nor encouraging others to take up arms, in Opposition to His Authority," the assurance of liberty and the enjoyment of their property.

Such assurances amused the British soldiers and made no impression whatever on the Hessians. The latter had been told in their native Germany that they could find private fortunes in America, so they looted the homes and barns of Tories as well as rebels. At Princeton, they plundered the library and museum of the University, even the planetarium, which was then considered to be the finest in the world. The Jerseymen bitterly regretted their previous cooperation with the British, and were in a good mood to "get even." In the American Archives, a letter written from this section and dated December 13th, 1776, describes authenticated instances of robbery and outrage.

For many reasons military conferences at the Thompson-Neely House, during December, 1776, were inevitable. The house was the river headquarters for the main body of the American army and Washington's ablest officer at this time, Lord Stirling. He and Washington had devoted a great deal of thought to the selection of that house as Stirling's headquarters. It was, first of all, the best house along the Delaware encampment to serve as the chief river headquarters. After all, it was to Stirling that Washington entrusted the difficult task of protecting the vital west bank of the Delaware in the area of the American camp. With Howe expected to cross the river at any time, this was the most important assignment in the Army. Besides its position on the western bank, the Thompson-Neely House offered another exceptional opportunity to Stirling. Its proximity to Bowman's Hill made it the most strategic and informative post along the Delaware. Stirling, who knew how successfully signals could be used from that vantage point, must be close to the "lookout of the Revolution."

Lord Stirling's Chamber

Thompson-Neely House, Washington Crossing State Park, Pennsylvania; Furnished by Bucks County Chapter, Daughters of the American Revolution

Stirling, his legs crippled with rheumatism, had limped through the house for the first time in mid-December to decide where he would sleep. He probably chose the bedroom above the west end because it offered the privacy he needed for the work to be done. The west room on the first floor might have been better for him, as he would not have to climb the stairs, but the sick and wounded men should be brought there for attention. Freezing, starving, stricken with retching and dysentery, they never could make the stairs, even with help. That lower room would better serve as a hospital for them.

As of December 22nd, 1776, the darkest period of the Revolution, for every ten of the rank and file who were fit for duty, seven were sick. Those figures alone tell a great deal about the army's weakness at this critical time.[5]

Stirling agreed with Dr. Rush's observation that hospitals "were the sinks of human life in the army." The dangerously overcrowded army hospital, located at Bethlehem, was an example. Infection spread rapidly, and many doctors, as well as their soldier patients, died.

At least, Stirling concluded, the poor devils in the Thompson-Neely House would get better attention than would their former comrades who were lying in squalor at the Bethlehem hospital. Yes, the west room on the first floor would best serve the needs of the sick. The entrance hall would be too public for him, and the "great" room, used for food storage and cooking, would have to do double duty as a council room. In that room there was the biggest fireplace and the most space for conferences.

One of the young officers quartered with Stirling at the Thompson-Neely House, Lieutenant James Monroe, has an interesting story. By December of 1776, Washington knew that he could count on Monroe as a scout, for Monroe's experience at Harlem Heights and on the retreat into the

[5]Freeman, Douglas Southall, *George Washington*, Vol. IV, p. 365.

Jerseys was to stand him in good stead for the task ahead at Trenton.

The picture of Monroe in the Thompson-Neely House, stooping as he stepped from the entrance hall into the "great" room, for he was tall and awkward, is worth noting. Monroe would observe with admiration, rather than envy, the graceful dash of another man, young Alexander Hamilton, who was quartered at the Chapman House. Hamilton was close to his own age and yet much more poised and sure of himself.

No doubt here at their headquarters, Monroe and his able friend, Captain William Washington, sitting close to the fire in the "great" room hearth, frequently talked far into the night. They must have shared exciting reminiscences about British contemptuousness at Harlem Heights, and they undoubtedly were anxious to "turn the tables" again and take the offensive against the arrogant British enemy.

The effort to carry on the fight for freedom had reached a foreboding crisis. This critical period may have helped to kindle in young Monroe the belief that led to the drafting of the famous Monroe Doctrine, the doctrine that was to influence American foreign policy up to the present day. Small wonder that in his famed canvas of "Washington Crossing the Delaware," Leutze chose Monroe to hold the American flag!

Chapter 7

Desperate Hour of History

The impact of those dramatic times in the fight for freedom left an indelible impression on another young officer from Westmoreland County, Virginia—John Marshall, a friend of James Monroe. Marshall, who later became the great Chief Justice of the United States, refers to his feelings in a letter to Justice Joseph Story:

... I am disposed to ascribe my devotion to the Union, and to a government competent to its preservation, at least as much to casual circumstances as to judgment. I had grown up at a time when the love of the Union, and the resistance to the claims of Great Britain, were the inseparable inmates of the same bosom; when patriotism and a strong fellow feeling with our suffering fellow-citizens of Boston were identical; when the maxim, "United we stand, divided we fall," was the maxim of every orthodox American.

And I had imbibed these sentiments so thoroughly that they constituted a part of my being. I carried them with me into the army, where I found myself associated with brave men from different States, who were risking life and everything valuable in a common cause, believed by all to be most precious; and where I was confirmed in the habit of considering America as my country, and Congress as my government.

General Washington knew he could rely on the passionate patriotism of his young officers and that they would react favorably to his daring plan for crossing the Delaware. He was sure of their enthusiasm. As Washington was well aware of Stirling's rheumatic condition, it is logical to assume that the Commander in Chief went to Stirling's headquarters for some of the important conferences during those critical days. He would have been the first to see the inadvisability of any unnecessary horseback rides for Stirling after that wildly dangerous and painful one his trusted officer made to Morristown on December 14th, for Stirling was thereafter practically immobilized.

History does not reveal what those two said to each other, but it is a well-known fact that each had the greatest respect for, and confidence in, the other's judgment. It is probable that Stirling reminded Washington of the words of British General Grant in the House of Commons on February 2, 1775, which he [Stirling] had actually heard: "The Americans could not fight," and "he [Grant] could undertake to march from one end of the continent to the other with five thousand men."

Grant's disdain of the Americans worked to their advantage in several ways. First, it had encouraged him to send the Hessian officers, who spoke little English, to the most dangerous British post at Trenton. Grant was so sure of the inadequacy of the Americans that he wrote to Colonel Rall on December 20th, "The rebel army in Pennsylvania does not exceed eight thousand men, who have neither shoes nor stockings, are, in fact, almost naked, dying of cold, without blankets and very ill supplied with provisions."[1] The description of the American Army was very apt, but the American troops had something more important than shoes—the leadership of Washington and Stirling.

Generals Hugh Mercer, Adam Stephen, and M. A. Fermoy had been put in charge of the vital defense area between New Hope, Pennsylvania, and Bordentown, New Jersey. Fermoy

[1] Stryker, William S., *The Battles of Trenton and Princeton*, pp. 334–335.

was stationed on the west shore of the Delaware, at Coryell's Ferry. Three miles below the ferry, Stirling had his command at Beaumont's Ferry. On down the river the guard stretched out—General Hugh Mercer at New Hope, General Philemon Dickinson from the Yardley Ferry to Bordentown; Colonel John Cadwalader to Bristol, and at the last outpost of southern defense, Brig. Gen. John Nixon at Dunk's Ferry below the Neshaminy. Washington was well aware that his regiments were stretched along twenty-five miles of river frontage, but he also knew that the line was too thin for adequate defense if the British were able to cross the Delaware.

Washington kept his head when all about him [except Stirling] were "losing theirs and blaming it" on him. The Commander in Chief had that quality of grim determination which was instrumental in turning the tide at the very height of its swiftness. It was that quality which inspired Rudyard Kipling's famous poem, "If." Dr. Borton Butcher, of Princeton, relates that provocative bit of information in his book, *The Battle of Trenton*.

At this point, Washington had to change the whole defensive pattern of American strategy. He knew that he had to take offensive action immediately, and yet, modest man that he was, he could not avoid wondering about his ability to win a resounding success at that critical hour. His military record up to that time had been weak and he knew it—Long Island, Fort Washington, Fort Lee—then the need for defense of his freezing troops along the Delaware.

Washington made up his mind to attack the British at Trenton, "in the most desperate hour of the life of the [American] army."[2]

As the officers gathered at the Thompson-Neely House for a vital conference, the very air seemed filled with excitement. In order to include Stirling in that important council, it is logical to assume that the officers met with their Commander in Chief at the principal headquarters along the

[2]Freeman, Douglas Southall, *George Washington*, Vol. IV, p. 322.

COUNCIL ROOM

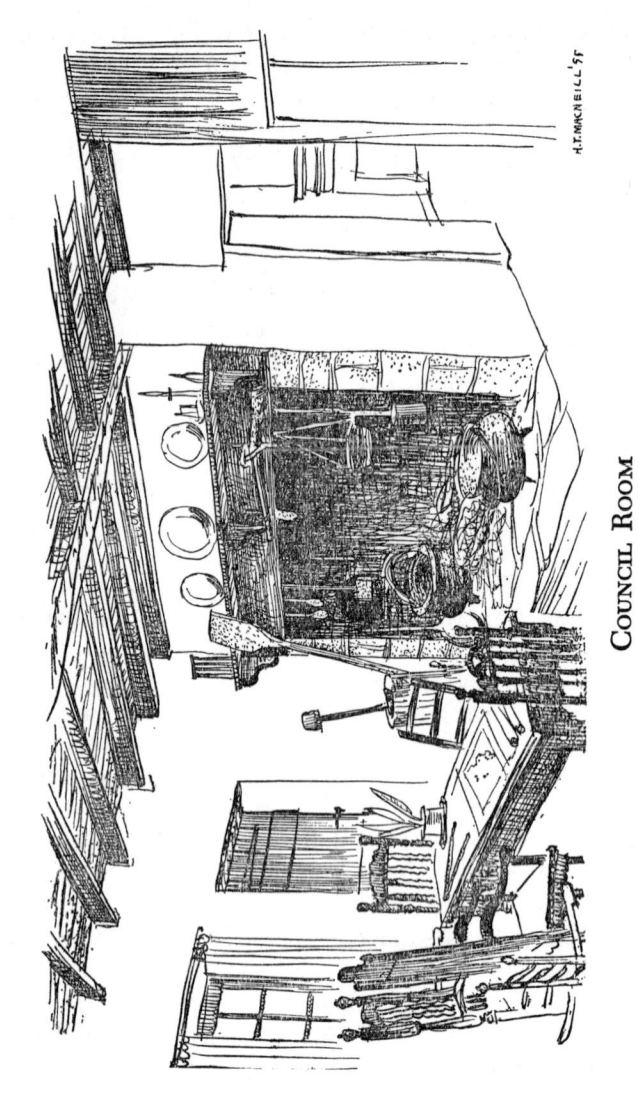

Thompson-Neely House, Washington Crossing State Park, Pennsylvania;
Furnished by the Author

Delaware.[3] Crowded with chairs, the kitchen became a council room; and the long table, usually laden with foodstuffs, assumed the dignity of a conference table. Stirling's maps and papers were already upon it. Washington added a packet of his own.

The sentry outside the south window peered curiously through the windowpanes. Another sentry was stationed at the north entrance. A third was posted at the river road and, far up on Bowman's Hill, the lanterns of its sentries gleamed through the bare trees.

The officers probably took their accustomed places at the long table in the center of the room. General Washington no doubt sat in the large wainscot chair facing the fireplace, and across from him Lord Stirling, his rheumatic back to the fire. At one end of the table sat Major General Greene, the highly literate blacksmith, who had become one of Washington's ablest generals. Major General Sullivan, a wealthy New Hampshire lawyer turned soldier, sat at the opposite end of the table.

To Washington's right we can picture General Mercer, and to his left, Colonel Henry Knox—a twenty-six-year-old bookseller from Boston. Near-by at a small table Captain Alexander Hamilton took endless notes. Standing at the north end of the fireplace were Generals Stephen and Fermoy, while at the south were two Colonel Johns—Stark and Glover—both of whom could be counted on for the difficult amphibious operations involved in a river crossing in the dead of winter.

At the southern end of the room, leaning against an old oaken chest, stood two young men, Captain William Wash-

[3]The Thompson-Neely House, restored by the Washington Crossing Park Commission, is now open to the public as an exceptionally interesting museum furnished with items of the Revolutionary period. Presided over by its able curator, Mrs. E. Linton Martin, it is open to the public daily from 10:00 A.M. to 5:00 P.M., Sundays, 1:00 P.M.–5:00 P.M.

ington[4] and Lieutenant James Monroe, who later were to be the heroes of that decisive battle.

An oddly expectant stillness pervaded the roomful of young men. Mercer was the oldest, fifty-two, and Stirling, fifty. Greene was thirty-four, Sullivan, thirty-six, Knox, twenty-six, and Monroe and Hamilton not yet twenty! Washington was but forty-four. All of them were young men desperately needed in that crisis.

Only the crackling of the giant logs on the hearth broke the silence. Washington's motions were, as always, deliberate as he separated the papers in front of him. He glanced toward the fire for a few seconds before he began to speak. His quiet assurance flowed into the room and reached the other officers, stilling the fears mirrored in their faces. Confidence was needed, for that critical situation was what Tom Paine had so aptly called *"The American Crisis, No. 1."* The cause for freedom was teetering on the banks of the Delaware and every man in the room knew it.

The reader is reminded of Marshall's comments on Washington: "He did not appear to despair and constantly showed himself to his harassed and enfeebled army with a serene and unembarrassed countenance, betraying no fears in himself and inspiring others with confidence."

Washington's "unconquerable firmness" was the rock upon which the American cause for freedom was clinging in the Thompson-Neely House, the night of that council of war in December, 1776. It gave convincing assurance to Washington's voice as he began to point out factors that the others already knew. The existing army, he explained, except for fifteen hundred men, would dissolve within a few days.[5] No one could be expected to join a failing cause.

A victory was the only way to keep the cause alive. Opinion abroad, sympathetic at first, was becoming derisive. Benjamin

[4]Related distantly, if at all, to General Washington.
[5]Marshall, John, *The Life of George Washington*, p. 69.

Franklin, on a record of rebel failures, could get no help from France. There was another important reason to strike at once. The American troops were still in possession of the boats along the Delaware, which meant they held the initiative until the river froze over. That particular December, unusually cold, indicated that such a freeze might occur any day.

Washington had to attack; he had to take a desperate gamble. He knew he must attempt a daring plan to surprise all the British posts on the Delaware at the same time! His words rang out in the low-ceilinged room, . . . "Christmas day —at night, one hour before day, is the time fixed upon for our attempt on Trenton. For Heaven's sake, keep this to yourself as the discovery of it may prove fatal to us. . . . Necessity, dire necessity, will, nay must, justify an attempt."

The hour of decision had come to the Thompson-Neely House. The officers began to leave. The sentry at the southern doorway watched them file solemnly from the house after the lengthy conference that followed Washington's announcement. He cupped his hands to his lips and blew his hot breath on numb fingers.

Only two—Stirling and Monroe—still talked by the fire. General Washington and his aide had disappeared into the west wing.

The Commander in Chief turned toward the hospital room to speak to the sick. Several of the patients stood up as he entered the room, but others, unable to rise, lay on their straw beds—some close to death, one dying at that very moment. Two of the men who were not so ill as their mates acted as orderlies. Only a few of the worst cases had mattresses; others lay on homespun remnants flung over straw. Several medicine bottles, together with a mortar and pestle, stood on the mantel next to a small medicinal scale.

In one corner of the room an old pine table held a scattered assortment of the pitifully few possessions of the sick. The ill men lay in a semicircle with their feet toward the fireplace in the center of the room, for it provided the only heat. A heavy smoke filled the air, because of lack of ventilation; at that time smoke was considered beneficial. The bodies of several of the men were covered with the hideous scabs of scabies. Sulfur and oil provided the only relief. In another corner of the hospital room stood a chest belonging to Captain James Moore of the New York Artillery, who lay nearby on his pallet. The eyes of that 24-year-old officer looked enormous and feverishly bright in his flushed face. No doubt he watched his Commander in Chief lean over a dying sergeant pushed close to the fire for warmth. Young Moore, fully aware that he, too, was seriously ill, turned his face to the wall, but Washington, ever observant, caught the expression on the captain's face. As he walked over to the dying captain he was thinking about Tom Paine's new pamphlet called *The American Crisis,* No. 1, that he planned to have read at every corporal's guard. The words would ring out for centuries—"These are the times that try men's souls —the summer soldier and the sunshine patriot will, in this crisis, shrink from the service of his country, but he that stands it now deserves the love and thanks of man and woman."

Washington put his hand on Moore's thin shoulder, "You are no summer soldier, son—no summer soldier," and he strode silently into the hall.

On December 23rd, General Washington ordered all troops to prepare and to keep on hand short rations. The watchword for the attempt was "Victory or Death," and victory or death it was to be, not merely death to the American troops but to the very cause itself. This was the first crisis in the early life of the new-found freedom. Appropriately, Tom Paine's pamphlet, *The American Crisis,* written in the horror and humiliation of the retreat through New Jersey, and published in Philadelphia on December 19th, was rushed to the camp. Washington ordered it read at every corporal's guard for he wanted his men to heed the words, "These are the times that try men's souls." Not a man who heard those fiery words could remain unstirred, not a man who was not braver because of them.

Washington gambled. He counted heavily on two basic psychological factors: one, the Christmas celebrant state of mind of the Hessians; and two, the courage of the shivering twenty-four hundred men who were with him at that critical moment. Who were those men, who were the first American soldiers? They came from Scotland and Germany, from Poland and Ireland, from England and France. They were not the deserters who had scampered off during the retreat through the Jerseys, many of whom went over to the better-paying, better-dressed, better-fed British army. The odd items of clothing that many of the American troops wore must have offered a startling contrast to the trim British uniforms and the smart bright blue dress of the Hessians.

The American soldiers were loyal to their country not because they couldn't desert; opportunities to do that were endless. They were not fighting for the glory, because their rags and losing cause made them objects of ridicule, not admiration. They were banded together because they believed in what they were fighting for. They had no lofty theories on liberty. They were fighting for the right to earn a living, to have a house of their own, to give their children an opportunity to grow up in a land of freedom and promise.

They had an ideal and a cause—both embodied in the faded banners they bore proudly. One, the standard of the Thirteenth Regiment, pictured a pine tree and a field of Indian corn against a buff background. Two soldiers in the uniform of the regiment, one wounded in the chest with blood streaming from the wound, were in the foreground. Under the pine tree several children were playing, and the wounded officer was pointing to them. His words formed the motto of the regiment, "For posterity I bleed."

Those men in the Continental Army were not only bleeding for their country, they were starving and freezing as well. In spite of all the problems which Washington faced, he,

GRAVES OF UNKNOWN REVOLUTIONARY SOLDIERS

Buried near Washington Crossing. In foreground, Tombstone Marking Grave of Captain James Moore of the New York Artillery, Who Died in the Thompson-Neely House Nearby on Christmas Day, 1776

courteous as always, found time to write a letter of thanks to the Pennsylvania Council of Safety: "Your collection of old clothes for the use of the army deserves my warmest thanks." The note remains as a pitiful and shameful commentary on the general apathy of Congress toward the situation.

Christmas Day, 1776, was bleakly cheerless. Ice was piled on both banks of the Delaware, and blocks of it were swirling along with the current. The river was dangerous for boat passage and yet not frozen solid enough for foot passage. Snow clouds piled up and the wind shifted to the northeast. Nevertheless, the operation must go forward regardless of the weather.

Washington, with about twenty-four hundred Continentals, planned to cross the river at McKonkey's Ferry, about nine miles north of Trenton. Brigadier General James Ewing planned to make his crossing directly opposite Trenton. About nine miles to the south of Ewing's position, Colonel John Cadwalader, acting Brigadier General, was supposed to gather together some eighteen hundred men and cross in the vicinity of Bristol. Ewing and Cadwalader were to cut Colonel Rall's line of retreat and so prevent Colonel Carl von Donop, Rall's superior in the South Jersey command, from bringing reinforcements from Mount Holly. Still farther south, General Israel Putnam promised some support against the more distant British outposts.

There was an ominous bite to the wind. Skies turned still grayer as the day passed and the wind shifted to the northeast. At the Thompson-Neely House there was one last duty to perform for young Captain James Moore, who had died that morning.[6]

Captain Moore was buried close to the river bank, beside

[6] The tombstone of Captain James Moore can be seen beside the graves of some of America's first unknown soldiers in Washington Crossing State Park. They lie beneath simple, unmarked headstones and a small American flag flies at the head of each grave.

the men who had gone on before him. His living comrades gazed toward the top of Bowman's Hill, then out across the ice-choked Delaware. Would they make it? Could they hope for the victory that would mean young Captain Moore had not died in vain? Washington prayed for the strength and guidance he would need for the crossing, that would be significant not only in the lives of these men, but also in the life of the new nation.

Early in the afternoon of that cheerless December day, the troops paraded behind a convenient ridge. Every officer's timepiece had been set with that of the Commander in Chief. As soon as darkness fell, the Durham boats, hidden behind wooded Malta Island since the retreat, were brought down to the ferry landing.

By 6:00 P.M., Washington had word from below Trenton Falls that plans were going awry. From McKonkey's Ferry he wrote to Acting Brigadier General Cadwalader at Bristol.

> Notwithstanding the discouraging accounts I have received from Colonel Reed of what might be expected from the operations below, I am determined, as the night is favorable, to cross the river and make the attack upon Trenton in the morning. If you can do nothing real at least create as great a diversion as possible.

The historian, Stryker, made the discovery of a diary of one of Washington's officers in which the tension of the hour is pictured:

> 6:00 p.m. The regiments have had their evening parade but instead of returning to their quarters are marching toward the ferry. It is fearfully cold and raw and a snow storm is setting in. The wind is northeast and beats in the faces of the men. It will be a terrible night for the men who have no shoes. Some of them have tied old rags around their feet, others are barefoot . . .

The snow suddenly changed to sleet. The men assembled at McKonkey's Ferry. In the darkness there Washington directed the preparations. Samuel McKonkey himself, a salty old character, enjoyed his exciting role in the crisis. Captain

John Blunt timed the boat loads. Colonel Knox shouted directions to the boatmen—most of them Colonel John Glover's seafaring men from Marblehead, Massachusetts. Those experienced sailors and fishermen, armed with rifles and clad in blue jackets, had to call upon all their skill that night in the ice-jammed Delaware.

Plans called for the completion of the crossing by midnight, so that the American troops could strike at Trenton before daylight. Even before Washington's troops had assembled at the Ferry, discouraging reports began to arrive. Cadwalader at Bristol was not able to assemble enough men to make an effective diversion. Besides, the tide at that spot added to the problems of floating ice and current. Adjutant General Reed had brought discouraging accounts from General Putnam in the Philadelphia area. But Washington did not falter. "I am determined to make the attack upon Trenton in the morning." Thus in Washington's "unconquerable firmness," lies America's greatest indebtedness to that great leader.

Other officers lacked the quality of determination. General Gates, without a word to his Commander in Chief, casually had left for Philadelphia. The crossing proved to be too difficult for several of the generals who had agreed to make it that night. General Cadwalader found it necessary to turn back at Bristol. General Ewing had tried to cross at Trenton and had failed. But General Washington crossed!

Conditions worsened; new ice began to form, adding to the dangers of the blocks already floating rapidly down the swollen river. The wind rose, and added to the difficulties even for the skilled boatmen from Marblehead. Loading eighteen field cannon on the Durham boats, with their narrow bows and sterns, was slower work than had been anticipated. Transporting the cannon and frightened and bewildered horses amid blinding snow and sleeting winds was a herculean task. Some of the first troops who had been ferried over the Delaware were falling asleep in the snow as they awaited marching orders. The warmth of their thinly clad bodies melted the snow, and they sank slowly to the frozen ground. Sleet and snow stung Washington's eyes as he peered across the Delaware. He knew that more of his men were sitting stiff and tense in the boats which bobbed laboriously through the floating ice and drifting snow. It was after 2:00 A.M. when the last piece of artillery reached the Jersey shore.

Historians and writers have given much credit for the success of the crossing to various officers and individuals. Credit is certainly due to every man who participated in the dangerous operation, but too little attention has been paid to the river skill and experience of the General himself. Washington had handled boats all his life; he had lived beside rivers —the Rappahannock as a child, the Potomac as a man. He knew how to navigate them in winter, for he was familiar with ice, tide and current. For the Delaware crossing, it is doubtful whether any other officer in the Army had Washington's uniquely parallel experience. At an earlier time, on a December night in 1753, he had attempted to cross another ice-choked river, the Monongahela, on a raft which he and a companion had constructed from standing timber. He had tried to use his pole to push the swirling ice blocks away from the raft, and found himself swinging out with the force of the swerved pole and falling into the freezing water. Only his exceptional strength enabled him to pull himself up on the raft. Little did the then twenty-one-year-old Virginia major, who was just returning from his first military mission, dream that that frightening experience was the best possible preparation for Christmas night, twenty-three years later!

An officer pictured Washington on the Jersey shore watching Glover's men trying to force the last boats through the floating ice, as sleet stung their faces. "I have never seen Washington so determined as he is now. He stands on the bank of the river, wrapped in his cloak, superintending the landing of his troops."

As always the Commander in Chief's calm face hid the turbulence of his emotions. Would the venture mean victory or death to his country's struggle for independence, to his reputation as a military leader, to himself as a man? The swirling river and ice threatened to overturn the heavily laden boats, but Glover's sailors met the challenge with remarkable skill. Jersey residents, anxious to "get even" with the British and Hessians for the treatment they had been receiving, watched the debarkation eagerly and even helped to haul the boats ashore. It was after 2:00 A.M., instead of the anticipated midnight, when the advance to Trenton finally began.

The snow had changed to sleet and cut the men's faces like a knife. As they marched toward Trenton, General Greene, who was leading one column of troops, sent a message to Washington, "Muskets wet and can't be fired." Washington's reply to the messenger was brief, "Tell your General to use the bayonet. The town must be taken."

By the time all the men and artillery were ready to move on to Trenton, Washington feared that the element of surprise had been lost, because it became evident that Trenton could not be reached before daylight. Under those circumstances, should he go on? There was only one answer for Washington, "victory or death." Sleet and rain fell on the faces of the men. It began to snow again. The Americans pressed on. It had been daylight for half an hour, and they were still a mile from Trenton. The first outpost, about a half mile from the town, was attacked, and six Hessians were wounded. The Hessian pickets withdrew in orderly fashion as Washington continued down Pennington Road toward Trenton. Washington later referred to the Hessians' skill by saying, "They behaved very well, keeping up a constant fire from behind buildings." The Hessian pickets were not all drunken sots, but "well built, athletic young men."

Word of the attack on the outpost reached Colonel Rall. He was urged to flee, but that contemptuous officer exclaimed, "Fudge! These country clowns cannot whip us." With the help of the weather, the "country clowns" seemed to be doing it. In view of the sleet and snow, Friedrich von Dechow, the Hessian major on duty that morning, had excused his regular patrol from making the usual rounds with a pair of cannon two hours before daylight. Once again, abominable weather proved to be Washington's faithful ally.

At last, the Third Virginia Regiment of the Continental Army led the brigade down King [now Warren] Street, Trenton. At its head were Stirling's two fellow officers from Washington's own Westmoreland County, Captain William Washington and Lieutenant James Monroe. In the face of a terrific fusillade, the two officers dashed out into the morning's fire to lead the charge on the cannon in King Street. Their successful capture of the cannon accounted in large measure for the swift victory.

The American troops marched triumphantly through the streets and the screaming confusion of Trenton. Rall's belated attempt to attack was halted halfway up King Street. In vain, von Dechow tried to make a stand against General Sullivan in the southern part of the town. The Hessians were hopelessly outflanked. General Greene, still feeling the sting of the loss of Fort Washington to the Rall and Lossburg regiments, knew the satisfaction of avengement as the same Hessian regiments surrendered in Trenton. The Knyphausen regiment fell back to the Assunpink Creek. Then Brigadier General Arthur St. Clair's brigade came to within a short distance of the trapped Hessians. There the Americans halted and, with a humanity unheard of in the warfare of later centuries, fired over the heads of their enemies. At command, the Hessians threw down their muskets, and the Americans jubilantly tossed their hats in the air . . . Victory in less than two hours after the first shot had been fired! Miraculously, in that swift attack not a single American soldier was killed!

Washington and his brave troops had proved indubitably that they were no "summer soldiers." They won a new respect for the cause for which they were fighting, a new faith in its future.

"This is a glorious day for our Country," Washington exclaimed happily as he rode down King Street in Trenton. The first report of the victory was sent from Bristol to Philadelphia by Colonel John Cadwalader. Shortly afterwards, Washington sent his prisoners to Philadelphia, to be paraded through the streets, their captured arms and colors carried behind them. No Tory could any longer doubt the completeness of the Commander in Chief's success. Reports of it rolled the full length of the British front, and filled the New York headquarters with apprehension.

Lord Stirling elatedly wrote:

> The effect is amazing; the enemy have deserted Bordentown, Black Horse, Burlington, Mount Holly and are fled to South Amboy.

The self-confidence of the British military leaders was shaken, while at the same time confidence in the American Commander in Chief spread, not only through the colonies but also abroad. The Americans, so long on the defensive, had expected a winter of constant alarm and fear of an attack on Philadelphia. Instead, it was the British who were to remain anxious, wondering what Washington's next move would be. The fabrication of British invincibility had been torn apart, and the tide of public opinion as well as of battle had turned. Cresswell, a visiting British journalist, on January 5, 1777, noted this change:

> The minds of the people are much altered. A few days ago they had given up their cause for lost. Their late successes have turned the scale and now they are all liberty mad again. Their recruiting parties could not get a man . . . and now men are coming in by companies . . .

The triumphant answer to the Trenton campaign slogan, "Victory or Death," echoed around the world. It stirred the hearts and hopes of the Americans and spurred on a steady determination to win eventual success at Yorktown.

The ball of military success had bounced from the gutter of defeat to the high wall of victory. From there it gained enough momentum to carry it to success at Princeton and through the difficult winter at Valley Forge, to ultimate victory at Yorktown.

No wonder that the authoritative British historian, Sir George Otto Trevelyan, wrote in *The American Revolution:* "It may be doubted whether so small a number of men ever employed so short a space of time with greater and more lasting results upon the history of the world."

This was victory in the most desperate hour of America's history, but it was more than a victory for America—it was the philosophical crossing from defeat and despair to hope and success. It was a triumph of courage and determination over suffering and humiliation. Every man, as well as every nation, usually makes just such a crossing in his lifetime.

That instant of crisis when the worst of the past poses for an instant on the brink of failure just as the promise of the future lends a steadying hand, was captured on canvas by Emanuel Leutze. In choosing this scene for his great historical work, Leutze revealed not only an appreciation of that most critical hour, but also an understanding of the never-ending struggle facing all the freedom-loving nations of the world.

Chapter 8

Climax of a Career

Emanuel Leutze showed good judgment as well as good showmanship in choosing the subject of what he hoped would be his masterpiece. In the minds of Europeans as well as of Americans, Washington's crossing of the Delaware was the turning point in America's struggle for independence.

Leutze knew that his canvas, "Washington Crossing the Delaware," must bring to life that dramatic epoch in human affairs. It should portray that moment in Washington's career when his thoughts, preparation and experience converge into an action destined for victorious achievement. The face on the canvas must mirror his leadership, and should reveal calm confidence to overbalance the fears and anxieties of the hard-pressed American troops. It must show nobility without aloofness and dignity without dullness.

Leutze made endless sketches of Washington before he was satisfied with the result. An original study of Washington, made by the artist, was found in 1934 in a Manhattan warehouse, where it had lain forgotten for ninety years. It was restored and exhibited by the National Academy of Design as a "Forgotten Masterpiece of American Art."

Leutze's pupils, Eastman Johnson and Worthington Whittridge, refer to a number of preliminary sketches of the painting, which they saw in 1849. Leutze may have made a trip to America before 1851, although that year is the first

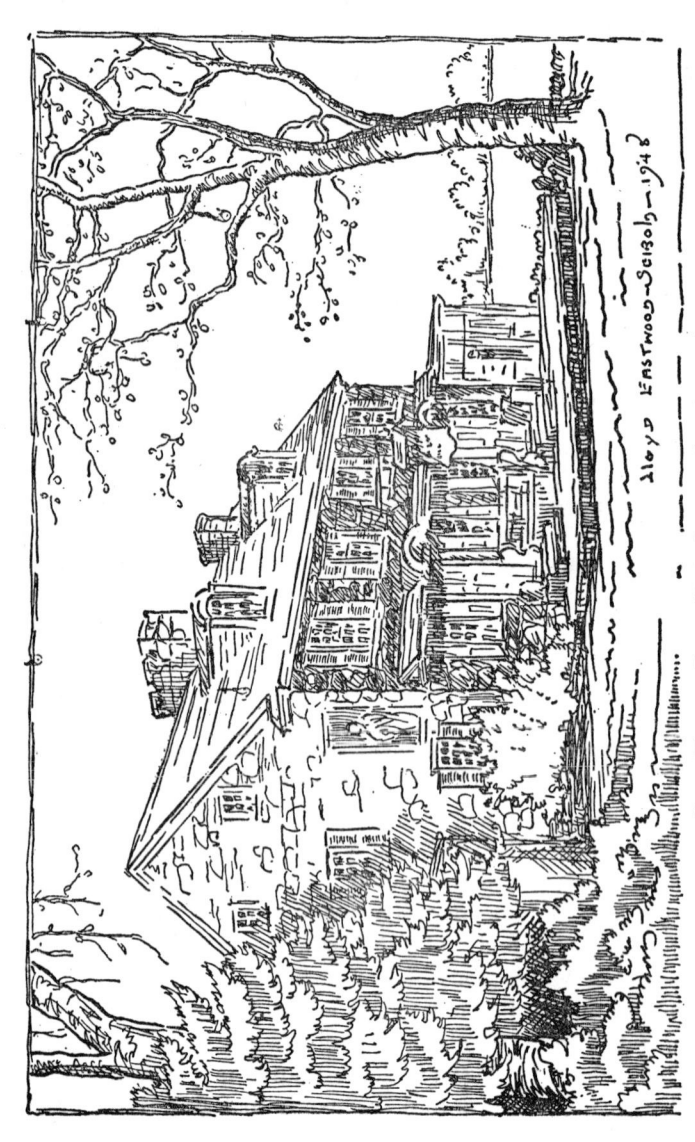

OLD FERRY INN (MCCONKEY'S FERRY)
Washington Crossing State Park, Pennsylvania

known date of his return from abroad. Albert Payson Terhune, the novelist, implies that Leutze visited this country sometime before his completion of the painting in 1851. He assures us that Leutze visited his grandfather, Abram Terhune, at Princeton, and there obtained some details for the painting. Terhune maintains that the husky blond fellow at the bow oar in Leutze's canvas was his grandfather, Abram Terhune.

Many people have located their ancestors in Washington's boat! It is an understandable ambition. One claim is irrefutably backed by fact, that of Euphemia Whittridge, daughter of Leutze's pupil and friend, Worthington Whittridge, who wrote that Leutze used her father as the model for the figure of Washington.

In a recent Associated Press Washington's Birthday release, the author was quoted on the subject of the men who were in the boat with General Washington when he crossed the Delaware. As a result, hundreds of friendly letters flooded her desk with valid-sounding claims about ancestors who made the famous "crossing" with Washington. Pride in this alleged association is both understandable and admirable. Stories have been handed down in families about the ancestors who "crossed with Washington," meaning with the main body of the Continental Army under Washington. Through the years this reference has been construed to mean "with Washington" in the sense of crossing in the same boat with him.

How many actually were in the boat with the Commander in Chief? Probably only a handful, for the American Army had more boats than it needed, so it is doubtful whether more than three or four officers and four or five men to handle the oars, crossed with their leader. The hundreds of descendants' stories at first seem outlandish, but a Mrs. Jane Jordan Hill, of Sutherland, Iowa, wrote a letter to the author which contained rather revealing calculations. She refers to an ancestor, a Josiah Jordan, as having been with Washington, and she adds, "Suppose those twenty men [with Washington] had an average of five children; now, after seven generations, this would mean 1,953,100 descendants! Perhaps that claim of an ancestor crossing the Delaware is more possible than you believe!"

The size of Leutze's first canvas was according to the artist, "twenty feet four inches by twelve, or nearly twelve feet in height." Each figure in the group had been sketched separately before it was assembled for the whole work. The central figure is, of course, Washington, wearing yellow knee breeches, high boots, a dark coat lined with yellow, a gray military cloak lined with red, and a black cocked hat. His sword hangs at his left side, and in his right hand he holds a spyglass. Washington's expression dominates the picture in the same way as the force of Washington's personality dominated the crossing itself and the ultimate success of the American Revolution. The Augsburg *Algemeine Zeitung* stated: "Washington is the chief figure of his celebrated painting—the look with which he seems to measure the shore is the subject of the picture, the rest is of little importance. He could not have stood or looked exactly like that. It is an ideal conception."

The distinguished American artist, Worthington Whittridge [Leutze's pupil], has given an interesting account of Leutze's work on the painting. In 1849, Whittridge, like many other American art students, went to famed Düsseldorf to further his art studies. On arriving there, he went to see his old American friend, Emanuel Leutze. Leutze's greeting was warmly enthusiastic, and he hastened to show Whittridge a small pencil sketch of the project he was then working on. It was only about six by ten inches in size, but the placing of the figures was substantially the same as in the completed picture. Leutze excitedly told Whittridge that he had ordered, just that very day, the enormous canvas that would be needed for his painting, some twelve by twenty feet.

For many days and long into the nights, Leutze talked constantly about his proposed painting. He worked tirelessly on the small sketches of the representative individuals that he was going to put into the boat and on correcting details of the Revolutionary uniforms. Much of the clothing seemed to consist of oddly assorted garments; when any of the art students questioned Leutze about this, he would patiently explain that, at that period in the Revolution, the weary American troops wore whatever they could find, and that only a few of the officers had presentable uniforms.

Leutze no doubt was the butt of much good-natured joshing about his "Washington Crossing the Delaware," and his avid interest in details of American history. It is doubtful whether anyone asked him why he drew Washington standing in the boat, since a standing position for a central figure was the traditional method of historical painting. However, questions about the type of boat were inevitable. Leutze's research had indicated that all types were used in the crossing, but that most of them were the sturdy Durham boats ordinarily used to haul iron from Durham Furnace near Easton, Pennsylvania, down the Delaware to Philadelphia. Those boats had been designed to haul fifteen to twenty tons of iron down river. Actually more than thirty men could be transported in one boat, which was usually about sixty feet long by eight feet wide, and supplied with eighteen-foot oars. The boats were somewhat like canal barges with narrowed bow and stern.

He also must have been questioned about the size of the ice blocks in the river. Leutze, however, remembered the Delaware very vividly, from the time he lived in Philadelphia, so he knew that huge cakes of ice piled up on its banks in winter. He wanted to convey to the onlooker an idea of the extreme difficulty of the crossing. He knew that the ice was at least thick enough to prevent Colonel Cadwalader from crossing to Trenton at Bristol on Christmas night, as planned, and also to keep General Ewing from crossing at Morrisville, Pennsylvania to Trenton.

Even though the American flag had not been officially

adopted by Congress at the time of the crossing in 1776, Leutze did not hesitate to use it to symbolize the new nation. There are examples of its use then. Leutze knew that both Trumbull and Peale, both of whom had served in the Revolution, showed it in their paintings on Trenton and Princeton. It was a known fact that when the American forces had been almost hopelessly weak in the previous January of 1776, General Washington had flown a flag as a rallying point for the demoralized men. Before the momentous crossing in December, Washington was sure to use every morale-lifting device he knew—from Tom Paine's heartwarming words to the flag which was the rallying standard for those valiant, freezing men.

In the final analysis, the flag, as Henry W. Kent, the understanding former secretary of The Metropolitan Museum of Art, stated, symbolizes "the cause for which Washington fought. The painting should be judged not on literal interpretation of possible historical inaccuracies but, according to the degree to which the artist achieved his purpose—that of representing an idealized event according to the artistic conventions of his time."

When the huge piece of canvas arrived at Leutze's studio, he could scarcely contain himself. He set to work at once, sketching the boat and figures in charcoal but without models, for he had difficulty in finding the right type of man to depict an American. German models were either too small or too short-limbed for his purpose. Leutze, remembering his previous experience with the "grapes" controversy in his Norsemen painting, and possessing a lifelong ambition to acquire critical and popular acclaim in America, would never have taken a chance by using Germanic types. The authority who sheds the most dependable light on the subject of Leutze's careful preparation for his canvas is Worthington Whittridge. Whittridge's recognition as a leading American landscape painter and a prominent figure in the art world deserves serious consideration. A long-time member of the

National Academy of Design, he became its president in 1875. Of Leutze's research and preparation, he said:

> Of all the artists I ever knew, I never knew one more conscientious and painstaking in all the details of his pictures especially relating to historic facts. He would spare no pain or expense in getting together veritable costumes and suitable models for his picture. . . .

It is Whittridge who claims that Leutze used his fellow American artists, including himself, for the work on which the artist was staking his whole future. Leutze had a wide acquaintance in Düsseldorf. He was the best-known American in that city, and wasted no time in trying to press every fellow countryman he knew into service. A friend of Whittridge, who had just arrived in Düsseldorf from Cincinnati, was asked to pose for one of the figures, almost before he had a chance to put down his suitcase! Another friend, a semi-invalid, was enthusiastically seized by Leutze. The artist tied a bandage around the invalid's head and immortalized him as the wounded soldier, whose face mirrored the suffering of the encampment along the Delaware. For the head of Washington, Leutze used his famous Washington mask made from the well-known bust by Houdon. For Monroe's, he used some of his own sketches of the hero of the Battle of Trenton and fifth President of the United States.

Whittridge himself served in two capacities, once as model for the steersman, and again for the body of Washington. It was difficult to find a model, either German or American, who could fill Washington's clothes adequately. Leutze, with his passion for details, had obtained a supposedly perfect copy of the uniform from Washington, D. C., through the influence of his friend, William H. Seward. However, since the models available did not properly fill out the uniform, Leutze pressed his tall friend Whittridge into service. Of this modeling experience Whittridge said:

I stood for two hours without moving in order that the cloak of the Washington could be painted at a single sitting, thus enabling Leutze to catch the folds as they were first arranged. Clad in Washington's full uniform, heavy chapeau and all, spyglass in one hand and the other on my knees, I was nearly dead when the operation was over. They poured champagne down my throat and I lived through it.

According to Whittridge, although German models were tried for the figures of the soldiers, none seemed to be satisfactory, so Leutze used Americans for all of them except one —a tall Norwegian.

A large part of the painting is occupied by the sky. Leutze mixed the colors for that portion overnight, and invited Andreas Achenbach, a fellow artist, and Whittridge to help him cover the canvas the following day. They all worked together to use the freshly mixed colors as quickly as possible. It was Achenbach who thought of the star and painted it in— a lone, almost invisible star, the last to fade in the morning light.

Once it was completed, did Leutze expect to sell his enormous canvas to the United States Government for display in the Capitol? There is no record that he did and no such intimation is referred to by the late Charles E. Fairman, in his work on *Art in the United States Capitol*. The author devoted many hours to a study of Congressional records in an effort to trace down that frequently reiterated statement but found nothing to sustain it. To verify those negative findings, she enlisted help from the staff of the Library of Congress. They reached the same conclusion:

> So far as we can ascertain, no agreement between the Congress and Emanuel Leutze, concerning the painting of "Washington Crossing the Delaware," was ever made.
>
> We have consulted the Office of the Architect of the Capitol, who informs us that no more information concerning this painting appears in Congressional records, or in their records.

Leutze worked day and night on his most ambitious canvas. Years of preparation and preliminary drawings lay behind the almost completed painting. What heartbreak the artist must have experienced when a studio fire seriously damaged the gigantic work! Leutze describes the calamity in a letter written from Düsseldorf on November 10, 1850:

> My picture of Washington [note his own emphasis on the work as a study of the man] is so much injured [by a studio fire] that I must give up all hope of being able to finish it without commencing it entirely anew . . . The picture was insured in the unfinished state for three thousand Thaler. The insurance company will (as according to their statutes the injured picture is their property) dispose of it by way of lottery for the benefit of the wives and children of the military of Prussia. Ten thousand chances will be made at one Thaler per chance. The copyright will be secured by me.

Leutze, energetic and determined artist that he was, began work on a new canvas at once. Here was born another controversy. Which of these works should properly be called the "original" painting of "Washington Crossing the Delaware"? The unfinished, burned work was put aside and the second "Washington Crossing the Delaware" canvas was completed. Later, the first one was repaired and finished, and remained in Europe, where it was eventually hung in the Kunsthalle in Bremen. In September, 1942, it was destroyed by Allied bombs. This Bremen canvas was *begun* first by Leutze, but the first "Washington Crossing the Delaware" *completed* by him was the famed canvas exhibited in the Capitol of the United States in 1851, and now on exhibition at Washington Crossing Park.

Apparently Leutze painted several smaller versions of the scene either while he was working on the huge canvas or shortly after its completion. One of these is owned by the Swedish Museum in Philadelphia. Another was the object of a search that went on for years. It was recently concluded by the author through the efforts of O. M. Scott, President of The Service Bureau Corporation, who located the painting. It is now owned by the International Business Machines Corporation and exhibited at Endicott, New York.

This second, gigantic work was even larger than the first one, being twenty-one feet four inches by twelve feet five inches. This meant two hundred sixty-five square feet of canvas and a weight of over eight hundred pounds. On its completion about six months after it was begun, it was promptly purchased by Goupil and Vibert, international art dealers, for ten thousand thaler, or about six thousand dollars, a fabulous sum for that day.

Leutze was always ready to find an excuse for a party and now he had a valid one. He held a gala affair at his studio to celebrate the completion of the work he had been dreaming about since boyhood. His guests always enjoyed themselves because their host was so jolly and obviously seemed to be having a good time himself. Red-haired Leutze, with his dog at his heels, towered above the crowd and he darted in and out laughingly among his friends and fellow artists, a glass in one hand, a cigar in the other.

He had every reason to be happy—he had a lovely wife, three healthy children, and, at thirty-five, had definitely "arrived" as an artist. The Goupil contract to purchase his painting had brought some financial security as well as the honor he had sought all his life—the approved plan to have his work exhibited in the Capitol of the United States. He knew that if the painting were exhibited in the impressive rotunda of the Capitol, it would mean future commissions for work and would serve as the key to success in his own country. It would be the climax of his career and would carry with it across the Atlantic the fulfilled dreams of the ambitious boy from Second Street in Philadelphia. It would even carry with it the boy himself, now become the most popular artist of the decade.

The message on canvas of such a vital moment in the history of man's search for freedom against tyranny could be understood by men, women and children everywhere. Was this not the message Leutze was trying to express? Prolific painter that he was, he left no written record of his beliefs. The best clue to his purpose is probably the brochure written to advertise the exhibition of his painting, in which he may well have had a hand. When Goupil and Vibert purchased the work from Leutze, it is probable that they asked him for some background material. Perfectionist that he was, no doubt he summarized some of his research for them. The brochure is quoted in part below. The author hopes that the reader will overlook the lofty and florid style, remembering that this was the mid-nineteenth century when patriotic sentiment was a sincere and honored emotion.

An Exhibition of Leutze's Great National Picture
of
"Washington
Crossing the Delaware"
Catalogue—Stuyvesant Institute
659 Broadway

Admission 25¢ Season Tickets 50¢

It was at the gloomiest time of the long, the weary, and unequal strife with the gigantic power of England, that the passage of the Delaware took place. The darkest hour of that protracted night of peril had then overshadowed the noble spirits who held in their keeping the welfare of their country—the freedom of the world, but they quailed not, for he who was their leader stood firm, and, amid all their peril, hopefully before them, and resting, under God, on his unequalled wisdom and fortitude, they then saw that the deepest night does indeed foretell the coming day, for the dawn of their liberty—dim, rayless, almost chilling, but still dawn—soon struggled through the gloom. . . .

In the midst of a storm of snow and sleet the first embarkation has been made; the advance of the army is seen in several boats stretching far into the distant twilight, and in the leading boat, with his eyes fixed calmly upon the desired shore, stands the Father of his Country. His attitude is earnest, determined, but in the excitement of the scene losing nothing of that unapproachable dignity, that air of benign supremacy, which was the striking characteristic of his presence. In his face no struggle is visible, care and trial have made it sad—the day and the hour make it anxious, but in its noble lineaments, feeble indecision and fluttering apprehension seek in vain for a resting place. Unyielding purpose sits firmly throned upon those lips, far seeing sagacity looks out undoubtingly beneath that thoughtful brow. It is the man prepared for any fate, but trusting in himself, his cause, and Heaven for the victory. He was at this time forty-four years of age, in the full ripeness of his vigorous manhood, the perfect maturity of his well poised mind.

In the stern of the boat by the side of an officer, sit two soldiers . . . In the wan, weary, . . . faces of these poor fellows, we read a tale of suffering and privation which would be heartsickening, were it not that we look there in vain for any tokens of a spirit crushed, or a purpose broken. In the midst of their sickness and misery they know no thoughts of submission, they dream not of purchasing health and comfort at the price of independence. If at first they lacked this spirit in themselves they have long since imbibed it from their leader. Such is character, and alas! in too many instances, such in condition were the daring spirits who crossed the Delaware to win the battle of Trenton.

The nineteenth-century prose set the stage for the exhibition, but the work itself elicited genuine emotion and acclaim. The public and the art critics of the day agreed in their enthusiastic response to the artist and this work.

Henry T. Tuckerman, the art critic, said,

. . . the sense of the adventurous and vivid sympathy with what is impressive in character and memorable in history seems to us the main characteristic in Leutze. He ardently sympathizes with chivalrous action and spirit stirring events.

He found "Washington Crossing the Delaware" "effective and impressive" and he summarized Leutze's achievement with a warmly patriotic tribute of the nineteenth century:

Leutze's heart . . . swells at the thought of great deeds and exalted suffering and can appreciate the majestic loneliness that plays like a divine halo around those who have deemed freedom and truth dearer than life and vindicated their faith by their deeds.

Even today the public could agree with the sentiments which the late Senator James Cooper of Pennsylvania, the lawyer and legislator from Philadelphia, expressed in Congress a century ago. Senator Cooper had served his state legislature as a Whig from 1843 to 1848, when he was appointed Attorney General. The following year he was elected to the United States Senate, where he served until 1855. Of the painting, "Washington Crossing the Delaware," he stated in the *Congressional Record* of April 8, 1852:

> A subject better calculated to awaken the patriotism of the American spectator can hardly be selected . . . Who that has looked upon that admirable picture, and contemplated that . . . composed yet inflexible determination which beams from the countenance of the heroic chief . . . has not felt his patriotism stimulated and the blood flowing in warmer and quicker currents through his veins?

It was the patriotism that Washington himself referred to in his "Farewell Address." Such loyalty and love of country is needed as much today, perhaps more, than when it was described by Washington in the unforgettable lines of his last message to Americans:

> The name of AMERICAN which belongs to you, in your national capacity, must always exalt the just pride of Patriotism.

Leutze had not only immortalized Washington's leadership in the turning point of America's struggle for independence, he had evoked for all men the sentiment of patriotism, so dear to the "Father of his country." He had indeed created a "Portrait of Patriotism."

Chapter 9

The Successful Years

In July, 1851, Leutze returned to the United States, as every boy dreams of one day returning—in triumph. Back at his old home, near the Philadelphia waterfront, his return was one of great rejoicing. His family had been confident of his success, and Leutze himself had the satisfaction of knowing that the doubters of his ability were forced to acknowledge the overwhelming success of the boy who had believed in himself. Leutze lived in an age when a successful artist was the most sought-after man of his day. He was the photographer, the reporter, the columnist and the stamp of social success.

Those were the fabulous fifties, when the country was expanding rapidly, and money was being accumulated just as quickly. The *nouveaux riches* wanted large houses and large rooms. They used big phrases and had grandiose ideas. Ceilings were high, walls were barren; and ideas on interior decoration didn't pop out of nearly every page of magazines and newspapers. The wealthy thought in terms of huge murals and large-scale paintings, preferably historical for their high-ceilinged rooms. All Americans, both rich and poor, were proud of their country and were delighted to have some significant scene of American history come to life on their walls. It was admired by their friends and worth a thousand words to their children.

Most of the art critics of that prosperous era were enthusiastic in their praise of Leutze's historical paintings. One issue of the *Journal of the American Art Union* stated:

> Leutze is always full in the expression of his thought. The promise of the sketch is more than redeemed by the finished work, every stroke adds to the completeness and power of the idea. His executive talent is greater than that of any other American painter. His form is always vigorous and rarely incorrect, his color is most pleasing and harmonious. There is no evidence of timidity and uncertainty in his pictures.

Another critic said:

> "Washington Crossing the Delaware" is simple and sincere without heroics. It almost illustrates the incident as it may have been conducted by men far too absorbed in the peril and possible failure of the enterprise to have any thought of arranging themselves in a striking theatrical group.

A contemporary example of a similar historic scene might be the magnificent one of the United States Marines raising the flag on Iwo Jima. Like that beloved photograph of World War II, the painting of "Washington Crossing the Delaware" aroused cheers and genuine emotion on both sides of the Atlantic. Leutze's theatrical sense must have made him happily conscious of the drama of his return to his beloved country with his masterpiece.

Congress in the mood of the times as well as the various state legislatures began to order huge canvases. For any era there is a man of the moment. In the fabulous fifties—the golden age of American art—it was Emanuel Gottlieb Leutze. The period of his reign in the art world was one of naiveté and sentiment, rather than the sophistication which ended with Gilbert Stuart's death in 1828. Prior to Leutze's day, historical paintings concentrated on fact, and the spirit of the work was often disregarded. Leutze's personality and patriotic fervor made him ideally suited to bring spirit to the rather heavy historical works of the period.

In the twenties and thirties of the twentieth century, the

era of the pseudo-intellectual, less discerning art critics sniffed disdainfully at the work of the expert craftsman. They labeled his skillful and disciplined style "unexpressive," but heaped praise on some *avant-garde* monstrosity. No doubt they would have found Charles E. Fairman's observations amusing rather than impressive. Fairman, the authority on art in the United States Capitol, said of Leutze, "The artist [is] distinctly an American and an enthusiastic believer in American principles."

Thoughtful critics now take a more mature view of nineteenth-century works. They recognize the fact that there is no such thing as art, per se. The art of any decade is the art of the standards and ideals of that era. Therefore, every artist must be judged, not by current standards, but by those of his own time.

American primitives have recently become fashionable. They are undeniably interesting and amusing. In those days they were executed, for the most part, by inferior painters who were not good enough to get commissions in the cities, and so had to look for work in the country. Such painters frequently drove wagons filled with paintings of the bodies of men and women. They then saved time and money for their patrons by painting on the heads for willing customers. These primitives are the exact opposites of the style of Leutze who grew up in three of the most sophisticated cities of the era—Philadelphia, Washington, and Fredericksburg. His portraits were done with insight and skilled technique. Frederick Fairchild Sherman, an eminent art critic, says of Leutze, "[his] portraits were singularly attractive, admirable in color and surprising in the degree to which they simulate the effect of the living presence."

When Leutze returned home in 1851, he knew that the triumphant period of his homecoming was the time to attempt to secure commissions for art work in the United States Capitol. But at the same time he was thoroughly familiar with the public use of art by the Government. E. P. Richardson, in his *Painting in America*, stated:

The impulse toward a public use of art of government has seldom appeared in our democratic society, when it has, the result has so often been an ironic comedy of misunderstanding, artistic frustration and popular disappointment.

One typically sad experience was exemplified by North Carolina's effort.

In 1818, that state had commissioned Thomas Sully to paint a picture of George Washington. The artist, without knowing the dimensions of the wall on which it was to be hung, painted a large, handsome canvas, which he called, "Washington at the Passage of the Delaware." It proved to be too large for any wall in the Capitol at Raleigh, and was rejected. Eventually it found its way to the Boston Museum of Fine Arts. North Carolina later commissioned Antonio Canova, the Italian sculptor, to make a statue of Washington. In 1820, it arrived in this country, but was also rejected as it depicted Washington, with an entirely unrecognizable face, and clothed with the armor of a Roman general!

Such disappointing experiences discouraged the state governments from considering further similar efforts, and the result was a general preference for portraits for commemorative purposes, rather than the more potentially controversial historical scenes.

After the War of 1812 the Capitol had been rebuilt and President Monroe had made meticulous plans for the Senate and House wings. Shortly before Zachary Taylor took office in 1849, Congress ignored the fact that the Capitol was under the direct supervision of the President and publicly advertised, offering prizes for Capitol extension plans. More space was certainly needed, and larger representation in the Halls of Congress meant that even the extra accommodations added in 1830 were no longer adequate.

President Taylor died only 16 months after taking office, and Millard Fillmore succeeded him. President Fillmore saw to it that his right of Capitol supervision was delineated in the first session of the thirty-first Congress. On September 30, 1850, Congress declared, "For the extensions of the Capitol according to such plans as may be approved by the President—one hundred thousand dollars to be expended under his direction by such architects as he may appoint to execute the same."

It was a long time before the needed extensions of the building became a reality, and ten years before Leutze's first commission for Congress materialized. His dream, however, had been going on for years. Ever since his first unsuccessful efforts at twenty-one, his chief ambition had been to execute a work that would hang in the Capitol. After the disastrous fire in the Library of Congress in 1850 had wiped out practically all Congressional paintings, the Library Committee was besieged by artists who sought commissions to do scenes depicting America's past and present. It was the custom at that time for Congress to grant permission for works of art to be exhibited in the Capitol by those who hoped thereby to gain Congressional interest and painting commissions.[1] Undoubtedly, this idea was in Leutze's mind when he wished to have his "Washington Crossing the Delaware" exhibited there in July, 1851, although he no longer owned the painting. Goupil and Vibert had purchased the work upon its completion. But by exhibiting it, he hoped to secure a commission to paint a similar work for the Capitol Building.

After the fire of 1850, Congress became newly interested in the idea of another group of historical decorations for the Senate and the House. Senator James Cooper of Pennsylvania spoke on behalf of Leutze, the "distinguished American artist." As a result of the Senator's interest, a resolution was passed that the Committee be instructed to inquire into the expediency of employing Emanuel Leutze to repeat his painting, "Washington Crossing the Delaware," for Congress. Although there are no records in reference to this inquiry, in the following February, 1853, another resolution was offered for "inquiry into the expediency" of commissioning three "native artists

[1] This practice was ended in 1868.

[one, Leutze] doing historical decorations for the Senate and House." This motion was considered and "laid over for the present." Actually, up to that time, only one painting had been purchased by Congress since the fire—a portrait of Henry Clay, which was presented to the House of Representatives at the time Clay lay on his deathbed.

Delays in the granting of commissions for art work occurred because of many political difficulties. There was a running battle between Thomas U. Walter, Architect for the Capitol improvements and the newly elected President, Franklin Pierce, who had appointed General Montgomery C. Meigs, as superintendent of work on the United States Capitol.

While he was in Washington in 1851, Leutze took orders from W. W. Corcoran, the nationally known art collector, for two paintings. These two, entitled "Milton Entertaining Cromwell," and "The Amazon and Her Children," proved to be two of the most popular works in the Corcoran Art gallery.

Meanwhile, Leutze had to return to Düsseldorf for an important reason—Julia was expecting their fourth child. Trevor McClurg Leutze, their second son, was born on December 5, 1851. Leutze's family seemed firmly anchored to Düsseldorf, at least until this newest child reached an age suitable for travel. Julia's reluctance to leave her home and family can easily be understood, for she had four children, and besides, she was sure of the devoted help of their adoring grandparents. With her husband's financial responsibilities to his mother and sister, as well as his own family, money had not yet kept pace with fame, for Leutze was a man of expensive tastes and expansive gestures. Many of the young artists who flocked around his studio needed money as desperately as he had when he first arrived in Düsseldorf. Leutze was sympathetic with their needs, and was quick to help with food, lodging and money. He worked endlessly for the cause of artists generally, and was instrumental in forming the general German artists' fellowship, the "Malkasten," known as "The Paintbox," which became one of the most distinguished artists' clubs in the world.

Actually Leutze managed to work on both sides of the Atlantic, for during that period he completed "The Battle of Monmouth," "The Departure of Columbus from Palos," "Rose of Alhambra," "Last Soiree of Charles II," "Light and Shade," "Wood Nymph," "Cromwell's Visit to Milton," "Titian's Sail on the Lagoon," "Return of Frederick II from Spandau," and "Defeat of General Braddock."

Leutze made several trips across the Atlantic to the United States before settling his family here permanently. He had a representative in New York and was successful in securing many commissions for work in the United States. He was a dominating force in the establishment of a new organization in Washington, known as the Washington Art Association. Horatio Stone was president; W. D. Washington, vice president; and the directors were Emanuel Leutze, Clark Mills, the sculptor, T. R. Peale, W. W. Corcoran, Ashur B. Durand, President of the National Academy of Design, and Robert W. Weir, Professor of Fine Arts at West Point Military Academy. The aim of the group was "to promote the progress of art through the coöperation of the artists and the citizens of the seat of government of the United States and to encourage and advance the Fine Arts." An outgrowth of this effort became the Washington Art Club founded later by W. W. Corcoran.

Leutze rode high on a wave of popularity with the public and the art critics of his day. He executed both historical paintings and portraits. His portraits of Nathaniel Hawthorne and Chief Justice Roger B. Taney won great critical acclaim. The undeniable genius of Leutze is evident in the Taney work. Both experience and study had qualified Leutze to perceive and depict faithfully the lines of age and suffering in the face of the man whose Dred-Scott decision foreshadowed the Civil War. The Supreme Court decision of 1857 held the Missouri Compromise to be unconstitutional, and Chief Justice Taney startled the North by declaring that Negroes had not been considered citizens by the framers of the Constitution, but rather as property and that only the states, not Congress, could regulate slavery.

The Republican Party, founded on the theory that Congress had the right to this regulation, recognized the dangerous import of Taney's decision. A young Republican politician from Illinois, Abe Lincoln, said that the Republicans, out of respect to the highest court in the land, would not fight the decision, but would try to have it reversed. Another Republican, the able William H. Seward, went further and denounced the decision as hateful and unconstitutional.

Taney, although applauded by his own constituents in the South, felt the sting of roused Northern opinion. His face in Leutze's immortal portrait consequently reflects the weariness and suffering of the decision.

After Leutze settled in Washington in 1859, his important plans for work in the Capitol seemed to be drawing to a climax, for he executed an astonishing number of paintings. "Anne Boleyn Persuading Henry VIII to Dismiss Cardinal Wolsey," "Scene from Paradise and Peri," and "Sergeant Jasper Saving the American Flag"—all three paintings had been completed in 1858. Within the next three years, in addition to numerous commissioned portraits, he executed "Lafayette in Prison at Olmüty Visited by his Relatives," and the superbly detailed, "Settlement of Maryland by the English under Leonard Calvert." He also managed to spend a great deal of time on preliminary sketches for a gigantic mural in the Capitol. Ever the perfectionist, the artist returned to Munich to study the wall-painting process perfected there by Wilhelm von Kaulbach, the outstanding artist in the field of mural decorations. The process is known as stereochromy, the base of which is a thin layer of cement composed of powdered marble, quartz, and limestone.

The title of Leutze's mural for the Capitol reveals its scope, "Westward the Course of Empire Takes Its Way." Careful craftsman and pictorial historian that he was, Leutze knew he must be exact about its details. He wanted the painting to reveal realistically the hardships faced by the pioneers bound for the West. He intended to dramatize the fact that their struggles were mental as well as physical. Facing the unknown, leaving behind the known, all those elements must be reflected in the faces of the pioneers. That episode was another "crossing" in the quest for freedom—this time across land instead of the Delaware River.

After innumerable delays, Leutze presented his sketches of the proposed work which was to be displayed on the west staircase of the House of Representatives. He was relieved and exhilarated when, on July 9, 1861, he was finally commissioned to begin his now-famous work on the mural.

Leutze was indebted in some measure to General Meigs for the opportunity to secure the commission. General Meigs took upon himself the responsibility of contracting for it. At the time there was a great deal of criticism because of the alleged extravagance, for Leutze set his fee at $20,000. A sharp disagreement arose with the Auditor of the Treasury over the accounting. A discrepancy in the dates caused the controversy since money had been advanced to enable Leutze to visit the frontier to study the scenes at first-hand and to make sketches from life.

According to Leutze's grandson, Admiral Trevor Leutze, his grandfather, not usually bothered by controversies or comments, was definitely upset by the criticisms of the fee previously agreed upon. The country was at that time in the early throes of the Civil War, and Leutze was motivated by a sincere desire to create a work for the Capitol of his country. Although the fee was to have been paid in gold, Leutze was willing to accept $5,000 in gold, and the balance of the money in the questionable greenbacks then in circulation.

Admiral Leutze explains that President Lincoln, a good friend of his grandfather, was grateful for Emanuel Leutze's coöperation and suggested that the artist might like to send that young son of his, Eugene Henry, still in Germany with his mother, to the United States Naval Academy. Leutze, extremely proud of the scholarship of his fifteen-year-old, was delighted to accept this suggestion.

While the vast mural was in progress, it was the subject of much controversy. Leutze by that time had become so well known in all walks of the contemporary scene that any work of his would be much publicized. In spite of some adverse comment, authoritative judgment called "Westward the Course of Empire Takes Its Way" the "finest fresco yet executed in the United States." It "put to shame the other tawdry efforts in that line of art in the Capitol." Such praise is not unexpected, because Leutze, besides being the best educated artist in America, had greater technical training and a finer power of conception than any other painter of his day.

One cold March day in 1862, two wen walked down Pennsylvania Avenue in the city of Washington. One man was exceptionally tall, thinner, and more stooped than the other. His deeply lined face and dark hair contrasted sharply with the ruddy complexion and red hair of his companion. Both men stepped carefully along the icy street. Frequently, people turned to stare and bow because those two Americans were outstanding men—each in his own field. One was Abraham Lincoln, the President of the United States, and the other was Emanuel Leutze, the popular and foremost painter of his day.

Quite a distance ahead of them, a woman, wearing a hat bedecked with feathers, slipped on the icy street and landed unhurt on her bottom. The two men could not resist a chuckle. The President turned and said to Emanuel, "She reminded me of a duck, feathers on *top* and '*down*' behind."[2]

The President and Leutze had inevitably become friends during the two years Leutze toiled over his work in the Capitol. Since the mural was the only work of art under construction during the Civil War, its progress fascinated President Lincoln. Both he and Leutze were amused by the controversies about the fresco. Of the work the Washington *Evening Star* eventually editorialized:

[2]This Lincoln story has been handed down in the Leutze family from father to son through three generations.

It has been severely criticized and often, but few who see it, however, can fail to feel its beauty and its power. It has received the homage of thousands as a truthful picture of the rugged road by which the star of empire winds its way to the far west and, in the face of the mother seated on the table rock, the feeling of resignation to a new life and sorrow for the old one left forever, there is the true stamp of genius.

President Lincoln also enjoyed chatting with Leutze about that fabulous new area, the West, and they talked at length about it as Lincoln sat for a portrait. This work, owned by the Union League Club of New York, is considered by many to be the closest approximation of the living Lincoln.

Leutze liked to report his experiences to the President as they discussed the current mining rushes spurred on by the discovery of precious metals in the vast new territories of Colorado and Nevada, and the probabilities that the Homestead Act would help to settle the West. The two men who had known great poverty in childhood and the real meaning of struggle for existence grasped the full significance of the new opportunity for many a poverty-ridden family. Though they always discussed the West at every sitting, inevitably their conversation would turn to the subject closest to them, the War.

Lincoln was well aware of the need for arousing a sense of patriotism and union during those desperate days and he was grateful for the enthusiastic response the people gave to current exhibitions of Leutze's masterpiece, "Washington Crossing the Delaware." It proved to be the number-one attraction at the New York Metropolitan Fair held in 1864 on behalf of the United States Sanitary Commission, the Civil War equivalent of the Red Cross.

Lincoln's discussions with Leutze about the Battle of Trenton and other historical events of the Revolution may well have been responsible for a comment Lincoln made in 1861:

... of [Washington's] struggles none fixed itself on my mind so indelibly as the crossing of the Delaware preceding the battle of Trenton. I remember that these great struggles were made for some object. I am exceedingly anxious that the object they fought for—liberty, and the Union and Constitution they formed —shall be perpetual.

Leutze's famous painting succeeded in telling on canvas what Edward Everett Hale was then accomplishing with words. Hale's *The Man Without a Country* first appeared anonymously in *The Atlantic Monthly,* in 1863. Its theme of patriotism helped to arouse feeling in favor of the Union during the war between the states. This was just what its author, Edward Everett Hale, the grandnephew of that early American patriot, Nathan Hale, intended it to do.

President Lincoln was very anxious to enlist the German-Americans in support of the war, and was aware of Leutze's influence with many prominent members of that group throughout the country. In this connection, T. Harry Williams in his book, *Lincoln and His Generals,* relates an instance of Lincoln's political astuteness, as well as his sense of humor. Lincoln agreed with his Secretary of War, Edwin M. Stanton, concerning a recommendation for several brigadier general appointments, but he added, "There has got to be something done unquestionably in the interest of the Dutch, and to that end I want Schimmelfennig appointed." Lincoln pronounced that name with relish. Stanton replied that several other German officers were more highly recommended. "No matter about that," said the President, "his name will make up for any difference there may be." Schimmelfennig it was, and Lincoln went off, repeating the name with satisfaction.

By the autumn of 1862, the outlook for the Union Forces had become grave. As Leutze worked tirelessly on his mural in the Capitol, General Robert E. Lee pushed on toward Washington. On August 9th, Confederate forces under General "Stonewall" Jackson had defeated the Union Forces at Cedar Mountain, and three weeks later they won another victory in the Second Battle of Bull Run. On September 4th, the Confederates crossed the Potomac and invaded Maryland.

Leutze of course did not know what the outcome of this bloody civil war would be, but he was sure that he wanted his son to enjoy the great opportunity made possible by President Lincoln, who had offered an appointment to the United States Naval Academy to Leutze's fifteen-year-old son. On October 9, 1862, Leutze wrote to the Honorable Gideon Wells, Secretary of the Navy:

> Sir: I have the honor to solicit an appointment as midshipman to the Naval Academy for my son, Henry Eugene Cozzens Leutze, who was born in Düsseldorf, Rhenish, Prussia, of American parents, in November, 1847.

Today in the National Archives Building in Washington, the yellowed envelope containing Leutze's application for his son's admission to the Naval Academy is on file. His residence is given as Washington, D. C., and on the outside is written, "Cheerfully recommended." The two sponsored signatures follow: "William H. Seward," and "A. Lincoln."

Young Eugene Leutze left his Düsseldorf home and a tearful mother in November, 1862, and manfully spent his fifteenth birthday, November 16th, alone in Ostend. He arrived at Boston on December 6th, where he was met by his joyful father and taken to New York and Philadelphia to meet his American relatives.

At home in Leutze's Washington studio, the artist fitted up a curtained corner for the boy's bedroom, and Eugene entered his father's noisy and exciting world. A constant stream of important guests flowed through the studio, but none made such a deep impression on young Eugene as the gaunt President of the United States, who greeted the youth with a never-to-be-forgotten affection and warm humor. Sleep was difficult for Eugene, because for hours after he had gone to bed, he could hear the loud discussions of the war that went on interminably in his father's always crowded studio.

On March 4th, young Leutze entered the Naval Academy,

which was then located at Newport, Rhode Island. The move from Annapolis had been made at the beginning of the Civil War, thus lessening the chances of capture by the Confederates. In October, 1865, the Naval Academy resumed its classes at Annapolis and Midshipman Leutze began his training there.

At the Naval Academy, Eugene was an immediate success in all classes except English. Since, however, he was far ahead of his classmates in mathematics, it was decided that he would spend all of his "math" time on English studies. He apparently had only one leave during his first year, a one-day visit to his mother in New York City. On October 31, 1863, Emanuel Leutze sent a telegram to Gustavus V. Fox, Assistant Secretary of the Navy: "Arrived safely. Can Eugene have leave for one-day visit to his sick mother in New York?"

Was Julia Leutze's illness actually the result of the recent trip across the Atlantic, or was she really suffering from homesickness? All that is known is that after completing his mural in the Capitol, Leutze had returned to Germany in 1863, in order to move his family back to America permanently. When he reached Düsseldorf, he was honored at a memorable affair. About one hundred-fifty artists and art lovers assembled at the Malkasten, the artists' organization he had been instrumental in starting. The group gathered just outside the Hof-Garten, the painters' clubhouse which was surrounded by beautiful gardens. When the unsuspecting Leutze arrived, he was greeted by music and old friends, who rushed to shake his hand, kiss his cheeks and hug him. Everyone was much affected by the return of the Düsseldorf hero. In response Leutze made a short and sympathetic address before all went to a sumptuous feast. Two of the artists had arrayed themselves, one as a Negro, the other as an Indian. Each artist serving him represented one of his paintings.

There in the illuminated garden, Andreas Achenbach, Leutze's old friend who had helped him on "Washington Crossing the Delaware," led the group in clever toasts and rollicking songs. They then presented Leutze with a delightfully humorous portrait of the artist stepping into a rowboat to return to America, that showed his red beard and his tousled red hair and above his figure was a reproduction of his famous "Washington Crossing the Delaware." Below it was a simple word—one with heartfelt good wishes. The word was "Abschied," "good-by."

Chapter 10

An End and a Beginning

Now finally settled in America, Leutze continued his furious work pace. He spent much of his time in New York, where, in 1861, he had helped to establish the New York City Artists' Fund Society. Its charter members included Leutze, Bierstadt, Worthington Whittridge, Eastman Johnson, and Thomas Hicks. At this time, his family ties with Philadelphia had been broken. His mother had died, and his sister, Louisa, had married for the third time, a Lieutenant Kehlhofer. Strained relations had resulted when the lieutenant barged into Leutze's office in the Capitol while the latter was busily working on his "Westward" mural. He wrote a coldly polite letter, May 15, 1862, to Louisa suggesting that his room in the Capitol was for his "government work," and that the lieutenant whom he admired for his "service to our country" might better have visited him in the evening at his rooms at 267 G Street, near 14th.

The following summer of 1863 was exciting, for the Civil War was reaching a climax. The Federal forces still felt their May defeat by the Confederates in the Battle of Chancellorsville. In late June, General George Gordon Meade had relieved General Joseph Hooker as Commander of the Army of the Potomac. John Slidell, Confederate Minister to France, was well aware that in this move lay the key to victory or defeat, so he offered Napoleon III $12,500,000 worth of cotton if France would send a fleet to break the Union Blockade. Napoleon considered this offer favorably.

The Union Naval Blockade had been slowly strangling the South. At the beginning of the war it was no more than a paper blockade with no actual enforcement by a real Navy. By 1861, the Union sailing vessels were out of date, and only twenty-four steamers were in service. The Government took action. Just as General Washington had confiscated the Durham boats when he planned the crossing of the Delaware, so did the Government buy every practical type of boat available: steamers, side-wheelers, clipper ships, tugs, and even ferry boats. Here was a real challenge—to blockade three thousand miles of coastline from Galveston, Texas, to Hampton Roads, Virginia, with nearly two hundred harbors! So effective was the effort that by the summer of 1862, the Confederacy held only the ports of Wilmington, North Carolina, Charleston, South Carolina, Mobile, Alabama, and Galveston, Texas. However, those ports provided an opportunity for swift blockade runners to trade with Bermuda and the West Indies.

By July of 1864, the blockade was tightening. Young midshipman Leutze, anxious to serve his country, reported on June 30, 1864, to the North Atlantic Blockading Squadron, and served on the *Monticello*. The ship's acting master, Henry A. Phelon, reported blockade runners on August 1st and 10th and picked up twenty-three bales of cotton thrown overboard from one as it made its escape. On August 26th, the Confederate *S.S. Tallahassee* managed to escape the *Monticello* chase and returned to the Confederate port of Wilmington, North Carolina. The *Monticello* crew was allowed prize money for picking up the cotton. For his services in the Civil War young Leutze, years later, received a meaningful badge, but, at the time a letter from his commanding officer to his father was all important. It read: "Your son performed his duties promptly and his willingness and aptitude to learn has won the esteem and respect of all my officers." That note of praise about his son meant more to Emanuel Leutze than all his art medals put together.

Eugene's four years at the Naval Academy had been critical ones in his country's history. The Union Army had won the war and General Ulysses S. Grant became the man of the hour. Eugene Leutze's father was the most successful of the many artists to paint Grant's portrait, and his portrayal of the Union leader, which he did in 1866, caught Grant's aggressive personality. It showed him in a natural and typical pose, with vest unbuttoned and a dispatch on his knee. This was General Ulysses S. Grant, the man of action, whose decisive leadership had won the Civil War. The public recognized the vividness of the portrayal, and as a result, Leutze received great critical acclaim.

The painter worked feverishly to fulfill all his portrait commissions. It was difficult for him to refuse pleas for sittings, or invitations to pleasant social functions. His buoyant spirit and bubbling good humor made him a much sought-after figure. The wealthy and socially prominent vied with one another in their efforts to be "done by Leutze." If he remembered those grim earlier years when he had desperately needed work, he never revealed his feelings. One fact is evident. He did turn down many sittings that would have guaranteed him very profitable fees in order to catch on canvas a significant man and the events of his time.

No facet of American life escaped Leutze's interest or his brush. His portraits of Chief Justice Taney had mirrored the legal conflict involved in the controversial Dred-Scott decision. In the literary world, his brush had delineated the charm and sensitivity of the literary lion of the period, Nathaniel Hawthorne, and he also illustrated fascinating scenes for the books of his friend, Washington Irving.

Hawthorne, the most popular writer of the early days of the Civil War, took a great fancy to Leutze. He described the painlessness of his sittings for the artist very vividly:

> I stay here [Washington] only while Leutze finishes a portrait which I think will be the best ever painted of the same unworthy subject. One charm it must needs have—an aspect of immortal jollity and well-to-doness; for Leutze, when the sitting begins gives me a first rate cigar, and when he sees me getting tired, he brings out a bottle of splendid champagne; and we quaffed and smoked yesterday in a blessed state of mutual good will for three hours and a half during which the picture made really miraculous progress. Leutze is the best of fellows.

In 1867, Leutze ably captured one of the most historic moments of the nineteenth century—a moment nationally celebrated a short time ago when Alaska became a new star in the national emblem. The purchase of Alaska took place March 30, 1867, and was immortalized by Leutze. In the painting, "Signing the Alaska Purchase Treaty," he depicted his old friend, William H. Seward, Secretary of State, seated by a large globe and looking across it at Baron de Stoeckel, the Russian minister, who stood on the other side of the globe. This meticulously accurate historical record is frequently reproduced in current history textbooks without any identification of the painter.

Few men have ever recognized the dramatic moments in American history as did Emanuel Leutze and few preserved them with such graphic fidelity. Another twentieth-century critic, Eugene Neuhaus, Professor of Art at the University of California, stated in his *History and Ideals of American Art* (1931):

> Leutze's versatility and productivity are amazing. He had the physical stamina of a Rubens and a spirit of enterprise which might have taken him to the far West to compete with men like Bierstadt, Hill, and Church; but his main interest in figures kept him within the field of historical pictures. It is his "Washington Crossing the Delaware" which has given him an enduring position as a national figure. Therefore petty criticism cannot discount the fact that the picture is an excellent academic composition, admirably balanced, possessed of much dignity and full of a spirit of adventure . . .

During 1867, Leutze worked on ambitious plans for a series of historical works, but the scene which for him held more significance than any other was that of his son's graduation from the Naval Academy in June of that year. Young Eugene Leutze, who graduated at twenty, reported for sea duty on the *U.S.S. Minnesota,* and in so doing fulfilled one of his father's dearest dreams.

The Leutze family, the father, Emanuel, the mother, Julia, and the children, Ida, Cornelia, Trevor and Eugene, whenever he was stationed near-by, was now part of the active social life in not one, but *three* cities. Leutze's commissions involved sittings and social contacts in New York and Philadelphia, as well as Washington.

He was in Washington during the summer of 1868 and, even in a city notorious for its extreme heat, it was exceptionally hot. The intense heat began in June and continued straight through July without any relief, so Leutze was glad that his wife was out of the city, handling some business for him abroad. He had been invited to head the famous art school at Düsseldorf, a position formerly held by the revered Schadow. Leutze was highly honored, but his work was in his own country, so Julia, with her graciousness and tact, became the emissary to handle the matter for him.

On a single day, Thursday, July 16th, the Washington *Evening Star* reported over twenty deaths from the heat. Day after day the temperature continued above ninety degrees. Leutze, although ailing, kept on with his heavy work schedule in his studio. He had a short time before received another commission for a work intended for the Senate Chamber. It was to be called "Civilization," and was said to have been most impressive in its conception. He had also made a pencil sketch of a historical painting larger than any he had ever before attempted. The proposed title had dramatic simplicity —"The Emancipation."

Because he had been singularly free of illness throughout his life, he was annoyed by symptoms of ill health evidenced on Saturday, July 18th. That day the temperature rose to ninety-five at 2:00 P.M., and continued to rise throughout the afternoon. The excessive heat had its effect on Leutze, and he collapsed in front of the Willard Hotel. Within a few hours, he was dead. Newspaper accounts gave the cause of death as "heat prostration and sunstroke." His wife was in Europe, his son on naval duty, but his daughter Ida was with him. Newspapers on both sides of the Atlantic reported the sudden death of a great artist who, at fifty-two, had become the "most successful painter of his generation."

The funeral service was held at his lodgings at 5:30 on Monday evening, July 20, 1868, and Leutze was buried at Glenwood Cemetery in the city he regarded as home. The Reverend Dr. Frickel officiated at the service, and Masonic honors were paid by the B. B. French Lodge.

Papers marked his passing by printing admiring editorials:

> In Emanuel Leutze's premature and shocking death, the ranks of American Art sustain a loss that will not be properly filled for we have no historical painter left behind who possesses his accurate education combined with his dramatic genius. He was an American by very early adoption and a Philadelphian by his father's choice. . . . He had a wonderfully rapid and inventive faculty . . . a kind of eternal youth. His great fecundity was his play, his sympathy, his friendliness, his welcome. The brightest of hearts of gold . . . leaves almost the whole art world of this country and Germany. His supreme good fellowship and scrupulous art study will remain as a mingled tradition of Leutze in the memories of artists in the United States.

Leutze had gone, but his love of country would be immortal. An editorial in one newspaper stated that his place in the world of art was marked by his "intense patriotism." That patriotism spoke to millions through many of his historical works and displayed its greatest power in "Washington Crossing the Delaware." However, Leutze was ever a practical man. He gave to the United States more than a heritage of immortal historical scenes. He gave to it a son whose career in the history of the United States Navy is a saga of achievement and valor. Like many other naval heroes, his service is unknown to the general public; but, within the ranks of the Navy's own department of public service, the record speaks for itself.

The competence and courage of Leutze's first-born son were tested early in his naval career. A communication of June 16, 1870, from R. B. Lowry, Commander of the *U.S.S. Severn* to Rear Admiral C. H. Poor, commanding the North Atlantic Fleet, reported on a collision that occurred when the United States ironclad, *Terror,* ran into the starboard bow of the *Severn* while at anchor.

> I wish to report the energy and promptness displayed by Ensign E. H. C. Leutze . . . a number of officers and men were forward on the gun deck when the collision seemed inevitable and they all left . . . with the exception of two officers who . . . cast off the stoppers and deck compressors thus freeing the cable and permitting twenty fathoms of chain to run out at the very moment of collision—which in my opinion saved the ship from being sunk . . . the tremendous weight and power of the *Terror* propelled by wind and tide at the rate of seven knots per hour . . . would undoubtedly have split the bow of this ship . . . I deem it my duty to call to your attention the promptness and coolness exhibited and the services rendered by Ensign Leutze.

At the moment of danger that young officer thought not of his own safety, but of that of his ship. There was the son of whom his noted father might well be proud!

In 1872, when the Navy was charged with the serious responsibility of providing surveying parties for the Nicaraguan expedition, it checked the record of young Leutze. The expedition would entail hardships, discomforts and would require officers who could be counted upon to use cool judgment no matter how adverse the circumstances; Lieutenant Leutze was chosen as Commander of Party Number One. The orders read:

> Much is necessarily left to your discretion and great confidence is felt in your judgment and that of the officers associated with you. I am sure that all that zeal can accomplish will be done.

Where zeal was concerned, America could always count on a Leutze, son as well as father.

The United States Government was interested in Nicaragua, because the Army engineers at that time thought that country provided the best possibilities for the development of a canal connecting the Atlantic and the Pacific. Eventually Panama was decided upon as the logical location for the canal. In the meantime, in January, 1873, Lieutenant Leutze was commended by his Commander, Edward P. Lull, for the "zeal, intelligence and cheerfulness with which [he] submitted to the hardships, discomforts and privations."

From 1874 to 1875, Eugene Leutze served on the Panama survey expedition. In the generally acclaimed success of the Panama Canal construction, the public was not made aware of the vital original studies that made the canal project possible. One of the important cogs in that basic work was Lieutenant Leutze, son of the famed painter.

Following the year 1875, young Leutze reported for special duty in charge of deep-sea sounding from Honolulu to Brisbane, Australia. From command of the *U.S.S. MacArthur* in 1876, he was put in command of a hydrographic party, United States Coast Guard and Geodetic Survey. Where his father exhibited precision in the delineation of a hand or a face, the son showed the same craftsmanship in his important work. On canvas as well as on the sea, father and son gave full measure of patriotic service. The commendation Eugene received on July 17, 1879, would have pleased his father, "Work which has nowhere been excelled in character and precision of results."

Leutze's skill in foreign languages—he wrote seven and could speak nine—had long been recognized, and the Navy called upon this skill of its versatile officer. On June 6, 1886, he reported for duty at the Naval Academy and, on September 1st of the following year, was made head of the Department of Modern Languages, a post which he held until June, 1889.

Leutze spoke Russian fluently, and it was he who translated

the specifications for the Russian ship *Variag*, built at Cramp Shipyard in Philadelphia for the Russian government. By 1889, he had been made a Lieutenant Commander and had assumed command of the *U.S.S. Philadelphia*. At that period of our country's history, naval activity and interest settled on an area of the South Pacific. Germany and Great Britain, as well as the United States, were interested in the islands. The three powers made an informal agreement to supervise the area, but a few years later each sent armed vessels to the South Pacific.

In the Central American area, tension had begun to increase during the early spring of 1898, and Commander Leutze, while in command of the *U.S.S. Alert*, requested that he be ordered to the front in case of war. Later, while in command of the *U.S.S. Monterrey*, Leutze was ordered to the relief of Admiral Dewey in Manila Bay. That action, according to John D. Long, Secretary of the Navy, "called upon patriotism, courage and the ability of all concerned." In February, 1898, Leutze landed with an armed force to protect the American consulate. His vessel was a prime factor in inducing the Spaniards to capitulate without serious resistance.

On June 7, 1899, a communication from Captain A. S. Barker, Commander of the United States Naval Force on Asiatic Station, stated:

> . . . the services of Eugene Henry Cozzens Leutze have been invaluable. . . . Admiral Dewey was very emphatic in his praise and I doubt that there is another officer in the service who could do better. If efficiency, service and untiring energy count for anything, Eugene Henry Cozzens Leutze is deserving of the highest award.

In 1901, Leutze was commissioned a Captain, and for the next several years, his experience and qualifications as an engineer were utilized in his superintendency of the Naval Gun Factory at Washington, and in services on various boards of inspection and survey.

While serving at the Washington Navy Yard, he supervised and planned a gala dinner aboard the presidential yacht, *Mayflower*. The affair was given by Charles J. Bonaparte, Secretary of the Navy, in honor of President Theodore Roosevelt. It was the first time in more than a year that there had been any entertaining aboard the *Mayflower*. Captain Leutze had not missed a detail that would add beauty and glamour to the affair. The approach to the vessel was brilliant with festoons of lights which wound from the mastheads to the decks. The simplicity of the decorations in the reception room reflected the taste of the man whose father had studied in Venice and was a great admirer of Venetian art for the only decoration was one large Venetian glass vase filled with American Beauty roses. In the dining room, spring flowers were featured, with white and purple lilacs and mignonette on the tables. Corsages for the ladies combined purple violets and orchids, while the men received boutonnieres of white violets. The sideboard gleamed with two handsome sterling silver loving cups flanking a huge punch bowl presented by the Russian delegation.

A typical Maryland dinner was served on the *Mayflower* by the Chinese staff, all clad in picturesque Oriental clothes of blue and white. The Marine Band and the mandolin trio supplied music for the distinguished guests.

The remaining years were filled with many distinguished social affairs, but Loutze was always an officer who loved the sea. In 1907, he requested that if he should be promoted to the rank of Rear Admiral, he would like sea duty. In July, 1908, with that hope in mind, he declined the position of Engineer-in-Chief of the United States Navy, as well as that of chief of the Bureau of Ordnance. The request for sea duty was denied because his services were more needed on land. He was asked, however, to serve under the direction of the Secretary of War on a committee of great importance. The purpose of the War Act for Defense, of June 6, 1909, was "for the purpose of manufacturing and issuing carriages for military seacoast guns of eight, ten and twelve inch calibre." Topping the list of those representing the Navy was the name of Captain Leutze.

On November 16, 1909, Captain Leutze retired as Rear Admiral, but continued to serve his country in several important posts, among the last being his supervision of the New York Naval Yard in 1912.

In 1931, in July, the month in which his beloved father had passed away, the son—naval officer, engineer, linguist, draftsman, and, above all, patriot—died. Rear Admiral Leutze's son, Trevor William Leutze, followed the traditions of his father and is a Rear Admiral, Retired, while his daughter, Marian, born at the Naval Academy, is the wife of Rear Admiral Gilbert Jonathan Rowcliff. The Rowcliffs live in Emanuel Leutze's beloved Washington, D. C., in a charming apartment, where a large Leutze portrait of two of the artist's children, Eugene and Ida, dominates the gracious living room.

Admiral Trevor Leutze lives with his wife in an attractive home in Winter Park, Florida. Several Leutze paintings adorn the walls of his home—one a portrait of Julia Lottner Leutze, Emanuel's wife, and another superb study of her with her small daughter Cornelia and her baby son, Eugene Henry. In the dining room hangs a portrait of Eugene as a Naval Academy midshipman. It is a wonderfully alive work with the young man's eagerness and vitality shining from the canvas.

Admiral Leutze has the height and light blue eyes of his grandfather. He carries himself erectly and, even out of uniform, has the bearing of his high rank in naval service. In World War II, he had charge of the building of the large supply depot at Norfolk. His was the responsibility for the erection and maintenance of a six-story, forty-acre structure.

Framed in his study is a commendation from the Navy for his engineering skill:

He performed meritorious service in connection with the design and execution of plans for the Fleet Supply Base at South Brooklyn and performed exceptional executive ability in the administration of that Base.

Near-by in a plain mahogany case are four rows of medals —his own and his father's. How proud Emanuel Leutze, both father and grandfather, would be were they living! His own medals had been received for many works of art, but one was for a work which also served his country, "Washington Crossing the Delaware." The grandson, Admiral Trevor Leutze, is proudly aware that this great painting will continue to serve his beloved country for centuries to come. The Leutze tradition of patriotism and inspiring service to country lives on.

Chapter 11

The Painting Everyone Knows

To produce both a son and a grandson who became Rear Admirals in the United States Navy should be a worthy patriotic achievement for any man. But Emanuel Leutze did more than that. He also bequeathed to his country its best-loved historical painting. On the basis of public interest, national newspaper coverage, and number of reproductions, "Washington Crossing the Delaware," by Emanuel Leutze, has proved to be the national and even the international favorite among American historical paintings.

This massive canvas has continued to fascinate the public ever since it was first exhibited in 1851. Throughout the proudly patriotic nineteenth century, it remained a popular favorite and continued to be the most widely reproduced painting in the country's history, appearing in most school textbooks and on the walls of many homes.

Its first owner and exhibitor, Goupil and Vibert [later known as Goupil and Company], had sold it to Marshall O. Roberts. At the latter's death, it was put up at auction with many of his other art treasures. Somewhat to the surprise of the European-minded art critics, an American work brought the top price of the sale, $16,000—a fabulous figure for 1897. It was purchased from the Roberts estate for The Metropolitan Museum of Art by John S. Kennedy, a Trustee and Vice President of the Museum. There, throughout the next fifty-five years it created more controversy than any other work of art. In presenting it to The Metropolitan Museum of Art, Mr. Kennedy expressed the hope that "it may assist in keeping alive a wholesome patriotism in the hearts of both the present and future generations of American citizens."

According to the late Myron C. Taylor, also a trustee, "No picture in the Museum has had quite the advertising this one has."

Although the Girardet engravings of this work no longer appear in American homes, according to *The New York Times,* its "popular appeal has constantly increased."

It is still the object of Sunday supplement controversies which, instead of detracting, probably add to its warm hold on the affections of the general public. [In regard to the writers who use these controversies to sell their articles, Lieutenant Winslow Humphrey, United States Coast Guard (Retired), wrote an interesting letter to The Metropolitan Museum of Art. He answered, point by point, a recent article that had attempted to prove inaccuracies in the painting. Humphrey then commented on "the wondering marvel of (the writer's) tremendous ego. It is regrettable that today we have allowed to spawn in this country a certain class of 'writers' who, under the guise of modern thought, have taken it upon themselves to debunk everything that stands for and represents authentic, historic and patriotic American history."]

A story of the Delaware River was published in *Holiday* magazine, September, 1957. The author gave an excellent account of the significance of Washington's crossing of the Delaware on Christmas night, 1776. Then he referred to the Leutze painting of the crossing as "stupid" because Washington was shown "standing up in the boat." In this criticism he revealed his own ignorance, for it is a tradition among painters of historical scenes to paint the central character standing when it is impossible to set him apart from the general mass by any other means.

In spite of the author's reference, the editor of the magazine devoted space to a color photograph of the painting now exhibited at Washington Crossing State Park. Readers who would not otherwise have given the article a second thought were moved to write letters of protest about the use of the author's derogatory adjective.

In the mind of the public, the great painting and the significant event which inspired it are inseparable. Leutze certainly showed both good sense and good showmanship in choosing this dramatic incident in American history for his most important work.

A recent Washington's Birthday article by Russell Landstrom, of Associated Press, was reprinted in hundreds of newspapers across the United States. The story began:

> What event, real or fancied, in the life of George Washington is he best remembered for?—several experts and quite a few simply curious people thought to undertake some research. They also interviewed visitors to the national shrine [Washington Crossing Park]. A sampling of public opinion was overwhelmingly on the side of the Delaware Crossing as the event for which Washington is best remembered.

In the early part of the twentieth century, the painting remained a popular attraction, but its reproduction in textbooks began to decrease. It seemed almost as though the earlier school emphasis on American history was lessening. Another factor in its disfavor was the propaganda rampant in World War I. During the winter of 1918, such words as "German," "Kaiser," and "Rhine" became ugly terms, staining anyone or anything with which they were associated. At the very height of anti-German feeling in this country, Dr. Bernard J. Cigrand of the University of Illinois, wrote an article for the Washington, D. C., *Evening Star* which appeared in an issue prior to Washington's Birthday. An alert newspaper editor is always interested in a new angle for a Washington's Birthday story so here was one tailor-made for 1918. The writer claimed that Leutze used the "Rhine" for his model of the Delaware, and "German soldiers" for models of the

Americans! The generally excellent article should be carefully evaluated, because the author was quoting the German caretaker of the Gmünd house in which Leutze had been born. Furthermore, in the winter of 1918, the "German soldier" idea is a bit obvious. This point has been entirely repudiated by a reliable "model," himself, Worthington Whittridge, who became one of the leading figures in American art and the president of the National Academy of Design.

The Cigrand story was sensational, and, as a result, was widely reprinted across the country. An article on the same material appeared in a March issue of *The Literary Digest* of that year. The public, inflamed by the words, "German soldier" and "Rhine," was in no mood to seek facts about either the execution of the painting or about Leutze's life and education in the United States, as well as his allegiance to it. Reverberations from that story account in some measure for the uninformed type of Sunday supplement controversies which still continue to appear about the famous painting.

Another factor in the painting's somewhat diminishing "star" during this period was the apologetic curatorial attitude toward it at the Metropolitan Museum. This presents a curious situation. Here was the most famed American historical painting of the nineteenth century, executed in the classical tradition of all great historical paintings which chose to impress in a dramatic manner, rather than photographically depict, a scene as it might actually have occurred. A good example of this old and honored tradition is Raphael's "Coronation of Charlemagne in the Vatican," which manages to convey a sense of majesty, and yet violates almost every historical accuracy.

This permitted symbolism would, in itself, explain Leutze's use of the American flag before its formal adoption by Congress.

Why then, did not the Metropolitan curatorial staff come to the defense of the work? There are probably several reasons. For one, they did not know all the facts of the case, and, because of the widely prevalent unfavorable notions about the artist's background, no one bothered to ascertain them. For another, the art of the mid- and late nineteenth century, like the architecture, was not fashionable among many modern art critics. Its realistic detail and disciplined style were deprecated by those who admired the increasingly popular, undisciplined, impressionist school.

Overlooked was the critical acclaim of such respected art critics as Samuel Benjamin and Richard Muther. The latter, in his standard *History of Painting*, brackets Leutze with Gilbert Stuart in discussing American art, by saying:

> First there have been portrait painters like Gilbert Stuart who acquired technical ability in England. Then there have been historical painters like Emanuel Leutze who, with the aid of experience gained at the Academy at Düsseldorf, recorded the events of American history in the most faithful manner.

While we may question the curatorial viewpoint for its lack of historical curiosity in regard to the Leutze work, we must sympathize with his problems. A huge frame added to the twenty-one-by-twelve-foot proportions. Admittedly, it occupied a great deal of wall space in the European painting galleries where it covered most of an entire wall. Why it was placed there instead of in the American Wing is not known. Perhaps, without full information on Leutze's background, the work may have been regarded as German rather than as American.

German art has been neglected for some years. Worthington Whittridge, the prominent American artist of the Hudson River School, stated that, "in American art circles, toward the end of the nineteenth century, it had become fashionable to deride the 'Düsseldorf School.'" He added:

> Writers and art students joined in the fray. They have not known what the school really was, especially in Leutze's day.

The "School" never really meant the influence of the professors of the Academy but has always meant the influence of the whole body of artists congregated there from many different countries.

The results of that prejudiced criticism of the "Düsseldorf School" inevitably besmirched the reputation of the American artist who was the most prominent figure identified with the once-famed art center.

Following World War I, Leutze's work was still regarded as unfashionable by the more superficial art critics. In the lush twenties, when wealthy Americans indulged in attempts to buy European culture, many tried the rewarding, though expensive, method of purchasing European works of art. Such works frequently found their way into the Metropolitan Museum. Many important treasures which provoked no controversy and, perhaps, no public enthusiasm either, could be exhibited in the space needed for the one frankly patriotic American work.

It is important to remember that patriotism, even the "wholesome patriotism" Mr. Kennedy referred to in presenting the painting to the Museum, was also unfashionable in the debunking twenties. This was the era when Rupert Hughes wrote controversial fiction, labeled "fact," about George Washington, the great hero of American history.

Some contemporary art critics dismissed Leutze with such comments as, "The best and the worst things that can be said about Leutze's works are that they were perfectly adapted to the taste of the time." One wonders what future generations may have to say to some of the formless daubs now bringing absurdly high prices as "modern art." Many of these impressionistic and surrealistic works become popular as the result of carefully planned promotional campaigns aimed at securing fabulous prices from wealthy patrons who fancy themselves as "forward looking." The popularity of Leutze's work was generated from the skill and craftsmanship of the painter himself.

Too many "modern" artists exhibit a lack of both talent and judgment. According to Dr. Elie Bontzolakis, a Paris physician who has treated about seventy abstractionists in the past ten years, they also show symptoms of poor mental and physical health. He states in a recent weekly magazine, *Arts*, that "the more abstract, the sicker they are."

Dr. Bontzolakis, a general practitioner, divides abstractionists into two classes, of which the first is by far the larger and includes the poseurs, the lazy, those seeking money and lacking in talent. This class, he finds, is rarely neurotic. It is the sincere ones who show alarming mental and physical symptoms, such as high blood pressure and dizziness. Other Paris doctors back up these conclusions. Bontzolakis makes no exception for one abstractionist who has gone farther than the rest. In *Time* magazine, March 9, 1959, he referred to Picasso, as "obviously an arteriosclerotic afflicted with hypertension."

Even such unsympathetic twentieth-century critics as Samuel Isham, recognize Leutze's abilities as well as his weaknesses. In his *History of American Painting* (1936), Isham quotes Leutze's technique as "smooth" and "dull," and his taste as "now seeming lamentably commonplace, although greatly admired at the time." He adds:

> He could put together a composition of many life-sized figures, all soundly drawn, in fairly accurate costumes and surroundings. . . . [His works] have not shown as great artistic vitality as that of less learned men with more feeling but one of his American historical compositions has fairly entered into the national consciousness and not unworthily. It is a good picture of its kind, well drawn, well composed, with the detail of the scene realized by the imagination until it carries conviction of its reality. Above all, the sentiment of the subject is rendered in such a way to be understood by all. It has taught to successive generations of school children, as textbooks could not, the high fortitude and faith of Washington amid discouragements and dangers.

Isham further states:

> Leutze represents the culmination of a certain type of historical painting in America. Pictures like his are still produced in Germany, and, with modifications for national taste, everywhere in Europe, but they have practically ceased here for causes which have been already suggested. Their execution demanded a training that was not to be had in America.

His painting of the "Fight at Fayal Against British Fleet in Azores, September 26, 1814," is accurate history as well as great art. It was lent from President Franklin Delano Roosevelt's collection for the United States Navy's first official art exhibition on May 8, 1940.

The nineteenth century was a period when every man, woman and child felt the "just pride of patriotism" to which Washington referred in his "Farewell Address." In the self-conscious adolescence of the America of the 1920's, the self-labeled "intellectuals" were apologetic about the still robust patriotism of the masses. The fate of "Washington Crossing the Delaware" at the Metropolitan reflects that trend.

In the European painting galleries at the Metropolitan it was found that the space occupied by the Leutze work was needed for a number of French pictures in the fabulous H. O. Havemeyer Collection given to the Museum by Mrs. Havemeyer in memory of her husband. In view of a rearrangement of the Havemeyer Collection, the Leutze painting would be "off exhibition" for some time. Apparently some members of the board felt that another museum location should be found for the Leutze painting. The appraisal of the situation by the Curator, Bryson Burroughs, was that all the halls, corridors and staircases had been searched to find a place for the Leutze work, but none could be located. As a last resort, it was suggested that in the attic between one of the offices and the electric fan there was a wall on which it could be hung, but, he added, the public would have to be escorted to the attic to see it.

However, a press release from the Museum in 1952 reveals an enlightened viewpoint and refers to this work as "perhaps our best known and best loved historical painting"! This later approach is exemplified in the comment of the art critic, Homer St. Gaudens, "Much of what was valuable in various eras is now regarded as inconsequential. . . . my yardstick is whether or not an artistic object met contemporary conditions. What is a failure today may be what is famous tomorrow or the reverse."

We can sympathize with the problems of Henry W. Kent, the Secretary of the Museum in the thirties, who had to interpret the academic viewpoint of the curator to a more realistic and public-relations-conscious Board of Trustees. He made a last-ditch effort by suggesting to the President of the Museum, Robert W. DeForest, that the painting might possibly be shown at the entrance to the American Wing. Mr. DeForest promptly sent a memorandum to Mr. Kent, directing that this suggestion be carried out. But Mr. Burroughs was not going to concede so easily. He replied:

> As it will take two men a whole day to reinforce the edges of the Leutze canvas and eight men working half a day to stretch and hang it, may we put it off until after the Davies show? It can be up by February 19 [or in time for Washington's Birthday, 1930].

Apparently Mr. Burroughs won his point, and Mr. DeForest's request was not carried out. "Washington Crossing the Delaware" was not hung for Washington's Birthday, 1930, or even the same event in 1931. But before February 22, 1932, it was hung after a controversy which is still remembered vividly at the Metropolitan.

During 1930 and 1931, when visitors to the Metropolitan asked to see "Washington Crossing the Delaware," they were informed that it was temporarily "off exhibition." Since there were times when various paintings were "off exhibition," this comment passed unnoticed until the fall of 1931. The nation at that time was preparing to celebrate the two hundredth anniversary of Washington's birth, February 22, 1732. Many institutions were preparing exhibitions of Washington paintings. The press then discovered that the most famous painting of him was not on display at the country's most famous museum. In fact, it had been rolled up, and stored in the basement for almost two years. The press services recognized a good controversy when they saw one and stirred the pot by sending out stories that were used across the United States. Headlines screamed out in large type that the beloved American painting, dear to every school child, was "gathering dust" in the Metropolitan basement. Comic strips and cartoons featured the painting as banished for the sake of "foreign art."

Even the conservative New York *Herald-Tribune* reported the irony of the absence of the painting, ". . . which had been reproduced more than any other Washington painting with the possible exception of Gilbert Stuart's portrait of 1796." The nationally syndicated columnist, H. I. Phillips, then at the peak of his popularity, devoted a memorable column to it. He wrote:

> "Washington Crossing the Delaware" has always been a great painting to me. It's worth more to the average museum visitor than six alleys full of masterpieces such as "Boy in a Blue Hat Rolling a Hoop," "Young Girl Peeling an Apple" or even Rembrandt's "Old Woman Cutting Her Nails." Anyone who would pan the painting would denounce the Lincoln Memorial on the ground that one of the hairs in Lincoln's head was not there on August 10, 1862, at half past three!

A number of newspapers dug into their files and, for want of other material, served up the old chestnut of World War I. One artist, Will H. Low, got into the act by repeating some gossip which, he said, was common in the 1890's, some twenty-five years after Leutze's death. The gossip was that Leutze had used a German laundress as the model for Washington. The artist, Low, who repeated the story, said that he got it from a painter who had studied in Düsseldorf fifteen years after Leutze's death, but Low refused to disclose the painter's name. Even on such flimsy hearsay evidence, the gossip was sensational enough to be widely circulated. It drew a withering and factual reply from Euphemia Whittridge, daughter of the well known painter. She repeated her father's statements that Leutze used a mask of the Houdon bust for Washington's head.

A few "fashionable" art critics expressed satisfaction that the painting was not hung, but the weight of public opinion was heavily in favor of it. The administration of the Museum felt the impact of public indignation. Apparently Mr. Burroughs believed that the widespread interest might present a good opportunity to get rid of the painting, but the wise Mr. Kent wrote a thoughtful commentary in reference to the Leutze controversy. It read:

> The attitude of a curator who thinks too much of the quality of the art and too little of the popular feeling towards what is an historic, public possession should not weigh too much. Wisdom in the case is more desirable than aesthetic judgments. It is my feeling that every effort should be made to show the picture in the Museum during the present Washington celebration. The question of its artistic quality could then be judged by the people themselves.... There is a public desire now to see the picture. It would be nothing more than gracious to comply with this desire.

William Sloane Coffin, the President of the Museum at that time, repeated the prejudice then currently fashionable in certain art circles, that the painting was "neither history nor art." However, pressure from some of his more realistic trustees finally induced him to issue a release to the press, which read:

> There is considerable discussion in the public press regarding the painting, "Washington Crossing the Delaware," by Leutze and the fact that it is temporarily not on display in the Museum. It is impossible to show all the paintings all the time and customary to change except in the case of great masterpieces. Such a change two or three years ago resulted in this picture's

being temporarily displaced to make room for a group of others. . . . "Washington Crossing the Delaware" cannot be classified as a masterpiece nor is it an accurate historical record. It is fitting and desirable that the picture be shown at the time of the Washington Bicentennial and in the Metropolitan Museum of Art in spite of obvious defects, as it has great interest for many accustomed to seeing copies in school books. Arrangements have been made to place the painting at the entrance to the American Wing during the Washington Bicentennial Exhibit held beginning February 16th. . . . The Museum has received requests from various patriotic historical organizations for temporary loan but no loan will be made prior to the conclusion of the exhibition . . . William Sloane Coffin.

A few days after the release, Robert E. God, the sole surviving executor and nephew of the donor of the painting, wrote the Museum:

Although this painting may not be the first rank artistically, still it is of very great importance and of widespread interest since its portrayal of one of the famous incidents in American history is familiar to and beloved by almost every American. It would therefore, I believe, be unfortunate if the painting were to be on public exhibit only occasionally.

The letter went on to suggest that if the Metropolitan did not care to exhibit it, why not have the painting hung "in some other place where it can be constantly seen by the very great number of people who enjoy it?"

Meanwhile, protests poured in from the "people who enjoyed" it and would like to see it exhibited where it could be on permanent display. One of the very first requests came by telegram from a politically astute governor who knew a popular issue when he saw one. This was January, 1932, and Governor Franklin Delano Roosevelt, of the State of New York, had his eye on matters of national interest, including the Presidency in the coming November. His forthright telegram assured the Metropolitan that the great painting would be given "excellent wall space in the Education Building of the State Capitol at Albany. It would be exhibited every day, except Sunday and viewed by thousands."

The Governor of the State of Washington also requested it on loan, as did several colleges, including the United States Military Academy at West Point.

Several states asked for the painting, California leading with four different requests. Historical societies, hotels, department stores, also a high school in Morrisville, Missouri, a G. A. R. post, the 107th Infantry, the Roxy Theater in New York City, and even an enterprising automobile salesman —all wanted it! The Museum politely turned those requests down but kept on file several of the most appropriate ones for further consideration. The patriotic organizations which led the protests were the Patriotic Order, Sons of America and the Daughters of the American Revolution. Individuals expressed their reactions in various ways. Owen Adams from Los Angeles, wrote, "One who would make Washington sit down crossing the Delaware would not permit Napoleon to stride the deck on his way to Elba, nor permit Lord Nelson to be lashed to the mast at Trafalgar."

Philadelphia resented the treatment accorded the work of their celebrated artist. The Philadelphia *Record,* January 8, 1932, carried the headlines, "Ousted Philadelphia Canvas Defended by Philadelphians." Mrs. Joseph B. Hutchinson, President of the Philadelphia Chapter of the Colonial Dames of America, and Charles B. Helms, State Secretary of the Patriotic Order, Sons of America, protested. The late Reverend Herbert Burk, rector of the Valley Forge Memorial Chapel at Valley Forge, said, "The painting has a message for the American people which should not be disregarded." A *Record* editorial summed up the attitude of the public:

> Fie upon the art critics. In our younger days almost every school room had its copy of "Washington Crossing the Delaware." On it the growing mind pondered as attention slipped from long

division and the dates of history. Few will refuse to admit a sneaking affection for the old picture, let the experts browbeat us as they may.

We may talk loftily of Cubism. We may gloat over Matisse and Picasso . . . But, by heaven, "Washington Crossing the Delaware" was REAL!

Time may yet avenge [Leutze]. Critics who sneer today may rave tomorrow. A hundred years hence the painting may be adored for its naiveté and charm and take its rightful place among our national archives.

A discerning editorial in the *Philadelphia Inquirer,* January 11, 1932, stated:

> What we all know is that this particular work has thrilled young people for many generations and that large numbers of persons are likely to be annoyed on learning that it has been tucked away in the basement. . . . Why must we be so critical of historical paintings? Grave fault has been found with West's noted painting of "Penn's Treaty with the Indians" and with Rothermel's "Battle of Gettysburg." And yet each of them served a purpose. We grant the poet a certain amount of license. Why should not the historical painter be given his allotment of tolerance? The Crossing of the Delaware depicts a great incident in American history and it has been the means of stimulating patriotism.

At the Washington Bicentennial exhibition, the painting once again turned out to be a chief attraction. Many more people viewed it than visited the exhibition itself.

The results of this success even brought about a change of heart on the part of some of the trustees. One of these who reversed his opinion, was the late Myron C. Taylor, later appointed by President Roosevelt as the first United States Representative to the Vatican.

> To many people who visit the Museum it would mean more than any other picture there. It impresses vividly upon the minds of those who do see it a great episode in the early history of our country. It is therefore an historical document. If the mass of

residents of foreign birth whom we have among us—now outnumbering us in a substantial way in this city—can gain a bit of inspiration about one of the occasions of great hardships that was endured in the struggle for independence, the better it will be for all of us. . . . Because it relates to an historic event of great interest, it seems to me that the Museum may well find a place to exhibit it, even though pictures of greater artistic value have to be put aside to accomplish it.

And so Leutze's great tribute to the memory of Washington won first place in the celebration of the two hundredth anniversary of his birth. It was a triumph for the painting, the painter, the people and for the Museum itself. Eighteen years later the canvas was shipped to Dallas, Texas, as the top attraction of an exhibition. From there it returned on loan to the very site it depicts, the Delaware, at Washington Crossing, Pennsylvania.

Through the generosity of the Trustees of the Metropolitan and the efforts of James J. Rorimer, its Director, the painting is still on exhibition at this historic park. After seven years of daily display, it continues to attract over one hundred thousand people a year. During the month of May, 1957, of 13,181 counted visitors, each state except Nevada, as well as thirty-two foreign countries, was represented. In this setting the famed work has enjoyed the most extensive and favorable national publicity it has ever received, and it has now entered upon the most gratifying period of its amazing career. With the wholehearted coöperation of The Metropolitan Museum of Art, the Washington Crossing Park Commission, the Department of Forests and Waters and the General State Authority of the Commonwealth of Pennsylvania, the Keystone

[1] Open to the public daily after September, 1959, dedication of the Washington Crossing Memorial Building. A recording will present the highlights of both the event and the painting which depicts its drama and significance. Other items of Americana will be displayed and a library of the American Revolution will be open to all visitors.

State, it will soon be featured in a new keystone-shaped Washington Crossing Memorial auditorium[1] erected at the Point of Embarkation. This historical document is now at the site of the key event of the American Revolution which it has immortalized. Here, in the most appropriate setting, "The Portrait of Patriotism," by Emanuel Leutze, will present its inspiring message to future generations.

Epilogue

The Painting Comes to the Delaware

It was a bitterly cold morning in late January, 1952. Murray Pease, Conservator of the Department of Conservation of The Metropolitan Museum of Art, New York, and I stamped our feet on the worn, wooden platform of the Railway Express Station at Trenton, New Jersey. The exertion did not overcome the biting wind, however, and we sought shelter behind a pile of baggage. Our faces felt stiff from the nine-degree temperature, so we talked little as we began our second hour of waiting for a special type of freight car to arrive at the platform.

Inside that car would be one of the most famous paintings in the world, "Washington Crossing the Delaware," by Emanuel Leutze.

The famous canvas was arriving several weeks ahead of schedule, which meant that the extensive alterations had not been completed on the small, stone church in which it would be exhibited. I could foresee many problems.

We had been unable to obtain the painting in time for our Christmas, 1951, celebration of the one hundred seventy-fifth anniversary of Washington's crossing of the Delaware on Christmas night, 1776. So we had reluctantly set our sights on Washington's Birthday, February 22, 1952. Uncertainty as to the painting's arrival had slowed preparations, and now here it was—about to appear a month before it had been expected!

As Mr. Pease and I waited in the almost deserted freight yards, I remembered that warm October day in 1951, when, on the spur of the moment, I had placed a person-to-person telephone call to Francis Henry Taylor, Director of The Metropolitan Museum of Art. I explained to him that Christmas, 1951, would mark the one hundred seventy-fifth anniversary of Washington's crossing, and asked him whether it would be possible to exhibit Leutze's painting of the event, at the very site of the crossing. Actually, I was surprised when Mr. Taylor told me that it might be arranged at some future time, but unfortunately, the painting was on exhibit in Dallas, Texas. Texas! I might have known! Whether it be a book or a building, a poem or a painting—if it has a significant place in American history, it is apt to turn up in Texas!

On the following day, I related the conversation to the startled members of the Washington Crossing Park Commission. Earlier, I had casually suggested this idea as a vague dream, but none of us had believed we might actually acquire the painting. And now, about two months later an exciting possibility was about to become a reality! We had received formal notice of the approved loan from Josephine L. Allen, Associate Curator in charge of Loans at the Metropolitan. The loan would be for two years, so the world famous painting which dramatized the historical significance of our Park would soon be here. But where would we display it?

There had not been time to erect a suitable "gallery." We had been faced with the considerable problem of deciding which building, if any, in the Park was suitable for the exhibition. The Old Ferry Inn? Too much attention needed for the one-hundred-fifty-year-old building. The Taylor House, which contained the Park Offices? Not enough space there for visitors. Someone suggested the Methodist Church near by.

Would its small congregation welcome such a dramatic addition? In the final analysis, the Metropolitan Museum and its insurance company would make the decision. There followed a number of conferences with the Secretary of the Museum, Dudley T. Easby, Jr., and the insurance company. They finally announced that the stone church was the only acceptable place. A number of alterations to the building were necessary. We wondered how the Board of Trustees and the parishioners of the Methodist Church would react to the alterations. A congregation of only ten or twelve members, as a tiny branch of the Yardley Methodist Church, had been worshipping there quietly for over a century. Before the erection of the building, all the little village of Taylorsville, later called Washington Crossing, Pennsylvania, needed was a church. The village was named for the Taylor family and by 1850, had about a dozen dwellings, a store and a tavern. Because it was on a regular stagecoach route, it was prosperous and accessible, but it lacked a church. Samuel Taylor undertook to raise money to build one. The church was begun in 1851 and dedicated four years later. Little did anyone dream that one day it would house a world-famous painting. This beloved work, within a few years after its arrival, attracted church donations sufficient to pay for the addition of an educational wing to house a Sunday school.

The idea of a famous painting in the church was startling enough. Murray Pease had decreed that it be hung "on the northwest wall, to avoid certain technical hazards including temperature and humidity, variations which would have been present on the wall exposed to the sun."

If this were done, Washington and his men would be headed toward the west, instead of east, toward New Jersey, a fact that was bound to evoke comment. But there were more immediate problems to consider. We would have to block windows, change the wiring and the lighting, remove an aisle of pews and hang new drapes. A letter, dated January 10, 1952, from Dudley Easby read:

> It is absolutely imperative that the entire wall area behind the painting be thoroughly water and weather proofed. This will

undoubtedly mean bricking up more than one window. In view of the northwest exposure of the wall and the fact that most of the storms come from that direction I cannot stress this point too heavily—in the matter of fire extinguishers we will have to insist on two foam type extinguishers of at least fifteen to twenty pounds capacity each . . . since the ordinary soda-acid extinguisher would probably work irreparable harm to the painting in the event that it became necessary to use it on or near the painting.

There were many other matters to think about. What of the wear and tear on the church carpets, equipment, and so on? We spent many worried hours in consultation with carpenters and masons. And exactly how was the Commission going to pay for all the items? The Park is operated on a budget worked out by the Commission and the Department of Forests and Waters of the Commonwealth of Pennsylvania. All items purchased must come within defined categories. Obviously none of the categories provided for velvet drapes and carpeting for a building not owned by the state.

Thirteen years of experience with red tape involved in attempts to obtain anything other than routine acquisitions had persuaded me to avoid any efforts through the state. I had set up a trust fund to purchase furnishings for the historic Thompson-Neely House in the Park. Why not borrow against this fund? One of the Commissioners insisted that the matter should be handled by the state. I reluctantly agreed. After innumerable conferences and delays, it was eventually Senator Joseph R. Grundy, who, continuing his long interest in our significant park, paid several painting installation bills personally and insisted that his generosity be kept anonymous.

All the aforegoing problems were ahead of me that bitter January morning. Up to that point the chief question had been whether the Metropolitan could solve the delicate problem of recalling the painting from Texas. It had been shipped to the Dallas Museum of Fine Arts for exhibition at the State Fair of Texas Mid-Century Exposition. The shipping problem for the twenty-one by twelve foot canvas to Texas was a formidable one. An eight-hundred-pound attraction could never be placed in a standard-sized freight car. The Conservation Department of the Metropolitan devised an ingenious plan, by removing the canvas from its stretcher and rolling it around a specially constructed wooden drum fourteen feet long and thirty-four inches in diameter. Before the drum was crated, a protective thin layer of hard wax was applied and a waterproof covering added.

In Dallas it proved to be a star attraction, and the year's loan had been extended into the following six months, when a letter arrived from the Metropolitan requesting the return of the painting for exhibition at Washington Crossing Park. Mr. Easby told us that we would not receive it by Christmas, but promised that we would have it by Washington's Birthday.

Texas had bid a sad farewell to "George," the affectionate term the Texans used for the painting. The Daughters of the American Revolution formed a guard of honor at the Dallas station. The American Legion and Boy Scouts of America paid a salute to "George," as he started on his long trek back to the actual scene depicted in the painting.

Would the freight train never arrive? It had been necessary for the Railway Express in Texas to use the type of freight car which could handle the huge crate. This was a special type with an opening at the end as well as in the middle.

At last the freight car backed into the siding, and the wide end door slid open. Murray Pease and I stepped inside. I don't know why I was so startled by the sight of the enormous crate. It looked like a gigantic coffin. The idea of this huge painting rolled on a cylinder and lying in a box was fantastic.

Soon a shivering photographer arrived and snapped some pictures of the crate with Mr. Pease and me, looking pained and half frozen, beside it. At last the crate was hoisted out of the freight car and loaded on a large moving van which we had ordered for the trip to the Crossing, since our own park truck was not large enough. Finally the strange cortege started toward Washington Crossing Park. The park truck held several members of the staff, including the late superintendent, Granville Stradling, and the present foreman, William Cooper. The van carrying "Washington Crossing the Delaware," crossed the Delaware on Route 1 via the Morrisville Bridge, because the bridge at Washington Crossing Park is too narrow for truck traffic, then we proceeded north along the river road on the Pennsylvania side to the Methodist Church, a mere five hundred yards from the actual site of the crossing.

Now began the task of getting the crate through the church doors. Advance measurements of crate and door proved inaccurate as the huge box could not possibly be carried through. The doors were not modern ones held by a hinge which could be removed by merely knocking a pin out of one end. This hinge was a hand-forged variety, not intended to be taken off. Finally, it was wrenched off and one door was removed. Cold winds swept into the little church ahead of the crate, which was still too wide for the opening! Here was another critical moment along the Delaware! The painting would have to be uncrated outdoors. After all, the crate and the painting could not be left unprotected in near-zero temperatures. Murray Pease appeared worried as he directed the men to open the crate. They pried open the lid and, with numbed fingers, carefully lifted the large cylinder out of the box. What would we do if even the cylinder would not go through the door? What about the insurance on the painting? The enormity of responsibility as the Commission member who had been given authority to handle this project, weighed heavily on my shoulders.

The men bore the cylinder slowly to the church door and gingerly edged it through. We all sighed with relief as they lowered it to the church floor. Then we huddled over the register to keep warm, and waited for the door to be replaced. It was now two o'clock.

Later that afternoon, Mr. Pease returned to New York and came back the next morning with two technical assistants. They donned white smocks and gloves and worked with brisk efficiency.

Mrs. Charles Harper Smith of the Washington Crossing Park Commission and the Reverend Jesse Eaton, then rector of the Methodist Church, joined me. By this time a few curious neighbors and half a dozen newspaper reporters and photographers appeared in the little church. While the park staff worked on the wall, technicians started to unwind the canvas. I watched with mingled emotions. Now I was about to see right in our own Park one of the most beloved and controversial paintings in the world. After a century of fame and travel, scorn and praise, "Washington Crossing the Delaware" was coming home to the scene it depicted.

It was unwound slowly from the cylinder onto the floor—first to appear was the bow of the Durham boat, the oarsman with the "coonskin" cap and, toward the center, the full-length figure of Washington. The small crowd stood tense and surprisingly still. As I saw Washington's commanding figure emerge, all my doubts and uncertainties about the venture vanished. I felt only the impact of Leutze's tremendous work. Finally the entire canvas was spread out on the church floor. Everyone knew now, if never before, why the painting had thrilled Americans for over a century. Leutze's technical skill leaped from the canvas. Here was a revealing picture of the period which Tom Paine called *American Crisis*, No. 1.

The spell was broken by the noise of men drilling holes to keep in place the hooks needed to hold the heavy canvas against the wall. With surprising ease, the canvas was slowly hoisted into place. Once there, its simple message of courage and patriotism glowed in the little church. The setting was too small, we knew, for a visitor had to go to the far aisle to appreciate the grand scale of the painting. But the spiritual setting was obviously right.

Now the Commission had to rush plans for draperies, carpeting and completion of the wiring. We anticipated traffic, of course, but we did not dream that in five years' time we would wear out two sets of rubber matting for the aisles and require refinishing of all the pews. Three Commission members coöperated actively in this phase of the work—Mrs. Charles Harper Smith, Thomas Elliott Wynne and A. Henry Gillam, Jr. All three people were exceptionally well qualified. Mrs. Smith, a graduate of The Academy of the Fine Arts in Philadelphia, was prominently identified with many art groups in that city. Thomas Elliott Wynne was the President of the Welcome Society and a well-known connoisseur of art objects and antiques. A. Henry Gillam, as manager of the Board of City Trusts of Philadelphia, had vast experience in all types of display and maintenance in connection with the numerous buildings owned and operated by the Board of City Trusts.

The Commission conferred with the Metropolitan Museum about the type and color of the draperies and were told these must completely block out the windows on either side of the unframed painting and harmonize with the canvas in color and feeling. We agreed on a rich red, but a hue that must not conflict with, or overshadow, the lining of Washington's cloak. When the draperies were finally hung, we were almost ready for our "D-Day"—Delaware Crossing Day, February 22, 1952.

The Martha Washington Garden Club, a local organization, offered to decorate the church appropriately, not only for the anniversary date but throughout the year. That group has either provided the arrangements, or scheduled them by other clubs throughout the exhibition of the painting. The Bucks County Federation of Women's Clubs offered to provide hostesses to help handle the crowds on week ends and this valuable service was rendered for several years.

In the Delaware Valley, February 22nd is a perilous time of year in which to plan a celebration because of the usual wintry weather, but we had no choice. The church could hold no more than two hundred comfortably, so loud speakers would have to be set up for those who could not get inside the building. The photographers also had to have some space. The *National Geographic* magazine set up an intricate platform, which enabled their photographers to sit above the crowd and make innumerable shots throughout the ceremony.

There was the usual flurry of excitement, the planning of the program, the customary problems of invitations when there is little available space for honored guests. Our chairman, Dr. Henry W. Turner, aged eighty-one, was critically ill, but his interest in the celebration never wavered.

We suffered through the inevitable guest omissions and substitutions. Finally, the 22nd dawned—cold and clear. I was scarcely awake when the telephone rang and one of the Commission members asked in an angry voice, "Have you seen the morning paper?" I told him I had not. "Well," he went on excitedly, "there's an article about the painting that states it is not the original, but only a reproduction! This is libel! You should bring suit against the paper!" With my mind busy with a hundred details, I could not permit myself to become too agitated. This was merely the first of many such comments. It would be some six years before I would have the answer to this century-old controversy.

When I arrived at the Park more than an hour before the scheduled ceremony, cars were already parked around the little church. The small building was soon bursting with a crowd almost twice its capacity. Representatives from many patriotic organizations were present—regents and members of the Daughters of the American Revolution, members of the Sons of the American Revolution, Sons of the Revolution, American Legion, Veterans of Foreign Wars, Patriotic Order Sons of America, Boy Scouts, Girl Scouts, Knights of Pythias, Descendants of the Signers of the Declaration of Independence, Colonial Dames of America and many others. Many visitors clustered outdoors around the loudspeakers. I spied our ten-year-old daughter in the audience and saw the genuine interest in her eyes as she looked at the big canvas. It was an interest to be shared by thousands of school children throughout the coming years.

Finally the ceremony was over, and guests and press had

enthusiastic comments to make on the event. Papers across the country carried favorable editorials. *The New York Times* reported:

> The painting, "Washington Crossing the Delaware," was placed on public view today close to the historic site it depicts—hope that the display of the painting at the scene of Washington's departure for his attack on Trenton will spark a new wave of patriotism was expressed by Mrs. Ann Hawkes Hutton of the Washington Crossing Park Commission who arranged for the loan of the canvas.

That night I tumbled into bed—tired but elated with a happy sense of gratitude for wholehearted coöperation on a challenging project. The next morning I was again awakened by an early phone call, and once more the voice was excited and angry. This time the speaker was a woman, who introduced herself by phone. "It's all very well to have the Leutze painting at Washington Crossing State Park. That's where it belongs, but what do you people mean by placing it in a Methodist church? You know perfectly well that Washington was an Episcopalian!"

Even after the Washington's Birthday event, visitors in great numbers continued to come to view the beloved historical scene. A typical cross section signed the guest register on a dreary Monday morning in November, 1954. I had gone to the church in order to meet a *Time* photographer who was photographing the painting for use in the fine arts section of a future issue of the magazine. During the hour we were there, six visitors came to view the canvas. While the photographer was setting up his camera and lights, I had an opportunity to talk with them. Two were from near-by Princeton, New Jersey, but the others came from Kansas (the President of the Kansas Historical Society), Cuba, Ireland, and India.

A curious cross section! The visitors represented different countries, religions, and races, but they shared an interest in the stirring and patriotic message of the painting.

In view of its location in Pennsylvania and within thirty-five miles of Philadelphia, it is not surprising that the greatest number of visitors live in the Keystone State. It is also to be expected that the second highest visitor group would come from the state bordering the other side of the Delaware, New Jersey. What *is* surprising, in view of its much smaller population, is the fact that the monthly visitor count from New Jersey not infrequently tops Pennsylvania's, especially during the month of May. Apparently the explanation lies in the large number of New Jersey school visitors during that month.

With New York City a mere ninety-minute drive via the new Turnpike, it is logical that New York should run third highest. But from this point on the figures are unpredictable. Tabulated figures have shown an average of close to one hundred thousand registered visitors a year throughout the seven years the painting has been at Washington Crossing Park. The registered figure could, in all fairness, be doubled to arrive at the probable actual count of some two hundred thousand, or well over a million visitors since the arrival of the painting at the church. Most public places, such as museums and shrines feel justified in doubling the number registered to get a probable visitor count. Even the tabulated count makes this exhibition in the small church one of the most popular historical attractions in the United States.

Keeping an accurate visitor record is a difficult task. On week days, there is no problem, since the traffic is sporadic and leisurely. The church guard has no difficulty in requesting visitors to sign the register. Week ends present a different problem. Lines form and many people, understandably, will not wait to sign. No attempt can be made to obtain the signatures of student visitors. The teacher in charge gives a total figure to the guard. Many times, in the inevitable excitement and crowding in the small church, the guard is so busy handling the traffic and guarding the painting that securing signatures is difficult.

At the church, we set up mimeographed sheets listing the names of states and foreign countries. Guards on the four-to-midnight and midnight-to-eight shifts could thus check home states and countries from the register. On the basis of a study of a year's figure (1956), totals were computed with the following results: Following Pennsylvania, New Jersey and New York, the next highest visitor count was Ohio and the fifth—the state farthest across the country—California! The sixth was no surprise—history-loving Massachusetts. Distant Illinois was in seventh place, ahead of nearby Connecticut, in eighth. Michigan was ninth, Maryland tenth, Florida eleventh, and Indiana twelfth. History-proud Virginia was in thirteenth place, and far-away Texas in fourteenth, ahead of near-by Delaware, fifteenth. Iowa and Kansas were in sixteenth and seventeenth places, respectively. Every state of the Union, except Nevada, was represented.

Of other countries, England had the highest visitor count, exactly one more than our neighbor, Canada. Next came Germany. Perhaps Leutze's German background explains Germany's place. South America was fourth, Holland fifth, Scotland sixth, Japan seventh, India eighth, Sweden and Denmark tied for ninth, and Ireland was tenth. Visitors have registered from such far-away spots as Arabia, Korea, Iran, Turkey, Indonesia, Ethiopia, Iraq, Israel, Thailand and even Russia.

One of the most interesting groups of foreign representatives was that composed of Eisenhower Exchange Fellows. The group, which arrived on March 17, 1957, included Enrique Pinedo, Chief of Investigations, Commercial Law Institute, University of Buenos Aires; Josef H. Jaegersberger, Chief, Quality Department, Boehler Steel Corporation, Austria; Kyriacos E. Zachos, Director, Greek Research Institute; Subramania I. Swayambu, Deputy Chief, Planning Commission, Government of India; Mordechai Max Levy, Assistant to President, Technion-Israel Institute of Technology; Mohamed Kailani, Senior Trade Officer, Ministry of Commerce and Industry, Sudan; and Yoichi Maeda, Professor, Tokyo University.

Statesmen, politicians, and celebrities from near-by celebrity-studded New Hope, Pennsylvania, find their way to the little church. The guard on duty is supposed to report the arrival of any important visitors to the Park office. The Park superintendent, Norman Fisher, who also serves as photographer, then takes pictures, and develops them for the Commission.

One day the system broke down when Helen Hayes, the famed actress, arrived unheralded, to see the painting. The guard, long an ardent fan of the first lady of the theater, stared in open-mouthed admiration, unable to utter a line about the painting, totally incapable of making the call to the Park office! The opportunity to photograph one of America's best-loved actresses against the backdrop of America's best-loved canvas was lost!

Generally, the most interesting visitors are just ordinary people—a young soldier from Fort Dix who, on his day's leave, sat in one of the pews studying the painting. An Iowa farmer came by bus from Trenton station to the New Jersey side of the Crossing and trudged across the bridge and south to the church to see the painting he had "wanted to see all my life."

Spotted among the visitors by an alert hostess from the Federation of Women's Clubs was one of the descendants of the painter, Emanuel Leutze. Contact with him resulted in receipt of some original Leutze letters.

The superintendent believes that his most unforgettable visitor experience occurred when he was conducting a Gray's Tour group from California through the church. The visitors were, for the most part, elderly, and they studied the painting with deep interest. After Mr. Fisher pointed out several factors about the historic incident of Washington crossing the Delaware, the group stood silent for a moment. One old man then asked, "Would it be all right if we sang one verse of our National Anthem?" They did so, eyes filled with tears, and the superintendent reports that even he and the bus driver had to brush back tears as deep emotion flowed through this little group of Americans standing reverently before the painting.

As the presence of the painting here became more widely known, there grew an ever-increasing school attendance. Typical of the development of school interest is the story of the Haddonfield, New Jersey, Junior High School. During the past ten years, I had talked to many groups about the Washington Crossing story. In early 1952 one of these was the Haddonfield Chapter, Daughters of the American Revolution. The group was interested in the possibility of taking some of the Haddonfield public school students to see the Leutze painting. I suggested that they first discuss the project with their school administration. When they did they encountered problems of schedules, time and transportation expenses. The Haddonfield D.A.R. solved the latter by taking over the cost of the bus trip as a chapter project. The principal, Donald Hart, then worked out a day's spring tour for the eighth grade as a part of the course in American history. In May, 1952, we had our first tour for this particular school. The group met at the Park, and the large class filled the little church. I told the students the story behind the painting and the various points of interest in the Park. A picnic lunch followed in one of the pavilions, and the students then went to their State Capitol at Trenton, New Jersey.

The continuing project has fostered a constructive relationship between the D.A.R. and the school administrators. Both have learned how to get maximum advantages from the trip with a minimum of disciplinary problems, one of which is to keep a guard posted between the picnic pavilion and the creek. The sparkling stream may prove too tempting!

A stirring moment has been added when the students visit the graves of some of America's first unknown soldiers near the historic Thompson-Neely House. The class president reads Washington's prayer to his classmates. Recently, the head of the Social Studies department asked each student to write an essay on his Washington Crossing trip. The following excerpts from several essays indicate what the painting means to the students.

F. Caroline Melhorn wrote:

To me, Washington's crossing is symbolic of what we of free nations should strive for—courage and faith in God. I feel, that on that night Washington had courage which no one can doubt, and a prayer in his heart. It is symbolic of what our great presidents have striven for, and of where our lesser ones have failed! In my opinion, we have many a "Delaware" to cross in order to insure liberty and prosperity to our descendants. Let us carry forth the "flag" as did Washington, even when hope seemed lost. This symbol is our greatest weapon against Communism and any other form of aggression which threatens our peace!

Mary Ann Test felt she had a personal message from the story:

These men were fighting for their freedom, but that was not all. It was *our* freedom, too. . . . I believe that these men have set a lasting example for all Americans. They did not give up because of . . . suffering and constant defeat, but instead, went on and fought for what they thought was right. I think that Washington and his men deserve a great deal of credit, because they risked their lives for freedom, both theirs and ours.

Prudence della Cioppa summarized a meaningful class response when she closed her essay with the statement:

When I got home that evening I began thinking over all I had seen and heard during the day. I determined to become a good citizen—the kind Washington and his men could be proud of.

Throughout 1955 the number of school groups grew astonishingly. Too frequently, we had no advance notice of their arrival. One May morning that year brought twelve bus loads from seven different schools to the small church at approximately the same time! That situation posed a real problem for the small Park staff and made guided educational tours an impossibility.

Soon after I was elected chairman of the Park Commission in January, 1956, the commission sponsored a round-table discussion with educators at the Park. We discussed the visual educational possibilities of the Leutze painting and other points of interest at the Park and also the means by which school tour scheduling could be worked out. School attendance with guided tours has increased steadily—not only from surrounding counties but such distant points as Wilkes-Barre and Stroudsburg, Pennsylvania, and Newark, Weehawken, and Avalon, New Jersey.

Opinions vary as to the age group deriving the most value from a visit to the painting. Most elementary schools teach American history in either fourth, fifth or sixth grade. In Junior High schools, it is usually taught in the eighth grade, and in the Senior High school in the eleventh. The artist, Stevan Dohanos, featured the eight-to-ten-age level in a memorable *Saturday Evening Post* cover featuring the famed painting. This is the age group which seems to respond best to the simple drama and excitement of the canvas. Children notice things which adults rarely see. One child pointed out the white charger on one of the boats in the background. "Did you know that was *Washington's* horse?" Another remarked about how worn the rope is as it hangs over the side of the boat. As for the coonskin cap worn by the fisherman sitting on the bow, that always attracts attention. We went through a Davy Crockett period when all small children thought they spied "Davy" in the boat!

Surely Emanuel Leutze would be delighted to know that the youngest of his admirers do not miss the details that mark him as a superbly faithful craftsman. He would be pleased as well by the vivid reality these details give to the story which continues to be inspiring to young people.

An eighth grader made an observation in her essay which we had never heard mentioned before. Wrote Patricia Harmon:

> As I was looking at this picture, I noticed the expressions on the men's faces. These expressions weren't of an unhappiness towards this trip, but of pride to serve under Washington, and most of all, to serve America. On looking closer, I saw that Washington was carrying a small token of Christmas with him—

a pin of two small bells with a bit of holly. It must have been hard for all of these men to have been separated from their families on such days.

The Commission has had the interesting experience of speaking to all age groups, from kindergarten to graduate students, and the most responsive and, surprisingly enough, one of the best informed audiences I've ever had was a third and fourth grade group from an elementary school in Plainsboro, New Jersey. They appeared unexpectedly at the church one afternoon, while I was speaking to a scheduled adult audience. We urged the school group to come ahead and see the painting, and I told them about it briefly. As I finished speaking, half a dozen hands waved to ask questions. They were pertinent questions and I tried to answer them. Their scope revealed the thoroughness of the preparation for the visit. They pointed out the bandaged heads, the red knuckles, and the white horse in the second boat. Again I was asked if I knew that was George Washington's horse.

This is the age when the painting has its most exciting story to tell. One question, which I always expect from any group, finally came. Why was there a flag in the picture when we didn't have a flag at that time? I asked whether anyone could answer that for me. A little girl held up her hand. "The artist wanted to show that Mr. Washington was carrying America across the river."

Was there ever a better explanation of the painting's message or its appeal for generations of Americans?

Bibliography

Adams, Randolph G.; The Dignity of George Washington, Ann Arbor, Michigan, 1932.
American Annual Cyclopaedia and Register of Important Events, New York, 1868.
American Archives: 5th series, Volume III, Washington, 1853.
Azoy, Colonel A. C. M.: Patriot Battles, 1775–1781, Washington, 1943.
Barnsley, Edward R.: Snapshots of Revolutionary Newtown, Bucks County Historical Papers—Volume 8, Doylestown, Pennsylvania, 1940.
Bill, Alfred Hoyt: The Campaign of Princeton, 1776–1777, Princeton, New Jersey, 1948.
Brown, Gilbert P.: Washington's Campaign in New Jersey, New York, 1932.
Bruce, Edward, and Watson, Forbes: Art in Federal Buildings, Washington, D. C., 1936.
Bryant, Louisa Munson: American Pictures and Their Painters, New York, 1917.
Butcher, Herbert Borton: The Battle of Trenton, Princeton, New Jersey, 1934.
Caffin, Charles H.: The Story of American Painting, New York, 1907.
Clement, Mrs. C. E.: Painters, Sculptors, Architects, Engravers and Their Works, Boston, 1892.
Clement and Hutton: Artists of the Nineteenth Century and Their Works, Boston 1879.
Congressional Globe, Volume 24, 1852.
Custis, George Washington Parke: Memoirs of Washington, New York, 1859.
Dictionary of American Biography, New York, 1933.

Dictionary of National Biography, New York, 1885.
Duer, William Alexander: Life of William Alexander, Earl of Stirling, New Jersey Historical Society, New York, 1847.
Duncan, Louis C., Lt. Col., U.S. Army—Retired, Medical Men in the American Revolution, 1775–1783, Pennsylvania, 1931.
Earl, Alice Morse: Home Life in the Colonial Days, New York, 1894.
Eggleston, George Cary: Life in the Eighteenth Century, New York, 1905.
Encyclopaedia Britannica, 11th Edition, New York, 1911.
Encyclopaedia Britannica, 1944 Edition, Vol. 13.
Fairman, Charles E.: Art and Artists of the Capitol of the United States, Washington, D. C., 1927.
Fielding, Mantle: Dictionary of American Painters, Sculptors and Engravers, New York, 1945.
Ford, Worthington Chauncey: The Writings of Washington, New York and London, 1890.
Freeman, Douglas Southall: George Washington, Volumes III and IV, New York, 1948.
Fuller, Major General J. F. C.: Decisive Battles of the United States of America, New York, 1942.
Garber, John Palmer: The Valley of the Delaware and Its Place in American History, Philadelphia, 1934.
Gardner, Helen: Art Through the Ages, New York, 1926, 1936, 1945.
Garrison, Lt. Col. Fielding H.: Military Surgeon, Washington, 1921–22.
Gibson, James E.: Captured Medical Men and Army Hospitals of the American Revolution, 1938, New Series 10.
Godfrey, Dr. Carlos E.: An address delivered before the Trenton Historical Society, Trenton, New Jersey, 1924.
Goolrick, John T.: Historic Fredericksburg, Richmond, 1922.
Greene, George Washington: Life of Nathanael Greene, Major General in the Army of the Revolution, New York, 1871.
Hammersly, Lewis: The Records of Living Officers of the Navy and Marine Corps, Washington, 1902.
Haven, Charles Chauncey: Thirty Days in New Jersey, Trenton, 1867.
Hazleton, Jr., George C.: The National Capitol, New York, 1897.
Henderson, Helen Weston: The Art Treasures of Washington, Boston, 1912.

Hutton, Ann Hawkes: George Washington Crossed Here, 1948 and House of Decision, 1956, Philadelphia.
Irving, Washington: Life of George Washington, New York, 1855.
Isham, Samuel: The History of American Painting, New York, Macmillan, 1927.
Jarves, James Jackson, Sr.: Art Idea, New York, 1866.
Kunstler, Lexikon 143, XXIII.
Larkin, Oliver W.: Art and Life in America, New York, 1949.
Lundin, Leonard: Cockpit of the Revolution, Princeton, New Jersey, 1940.
Marshall, John: Life of Washington, Philadelphia, 1836.
Middleton, William Shainline: Medicine at Valley Forge, Annals of Medical History, Third Series, Volume III, 1941.
Muther, Richard: The History of Modern Painting, New York, 1907.
Owen, Col. William O.: The Medical Department of the United States Army During the Period of the Revolution, New York, 1920.
Packard, Dr. Francis R.: Care of the Sick and Wounded in the War of the Revolution, North Carolina Medical Journal, Volume 43, 1899.
Parry, Edwin S.: Betsy Ross—Quaker Rebel, Philadelphia, 1930.
Pearson, Hasketh: Tom Paine, Friend of Mankind, New York, 1937.
Pennsylvania Archives, 1760–76, Volume IV, Philadelphia, 1853.
Pennsylvania: Coll. 6.
Quarterly Journal, New York Historical Association, July, 1928.
Records of the Columbia Historical Society, Washington, D. C., Vol. 24.
St. Gaudens, Homer: The American Artist and His Times, New York, 1941.
Sawyer, J. D.: Washington Portraits, 1927.
Scott, J. E., M.D.: Historic Account of Bowman's Hill, Bucks County Historical Society, Volume IV, Doylestown, Pennsylvania, 1913.
Secret Journals of Congress 2, 1775–81.
Sherman, Frederic Fairchild: Early American Painting, New York, 1932.
Stryker, William S.: The Battles of Trenton and Princeton, Boston and New York, 1898.
Taylor, David: Lights Across the Delaware, Philadelphia, 1954.
Thacher, James, M.D.: A Military Journal, Boston, 1823.

Trevelyan, Right Honorable Sir George Otto, Bart: The American Revolution, London, New York, and Bombay, 1903.
Tuckerman, Henry T.: Book of the Artists, New York, 1867.
Virginia Magazine of History and Biography, Germans in Virginia, Vol. 10, October, 1902.
Washington, George: Letters, 1776–1783, London, 1796.
Watson, Forbes: A Perspective of American Murals.
White, Joseph: An Account of the Battles of Trenton and Princeton, Charlestown, 1833.
Wilkerson, Gen. James: Memoirs of My Own Times, Philadelphia, 1816.
Wilstach, Paul: Mt. Vernon, Washington's Home and the National Shrine, New York, 1916.

Index

Abraham Lincoln, anecdote, 127
  appoints Leutze's son to Naval Academy, 130
  Battle of Trenton comments, 128–129
  Dred Scott Decision, 125
  friendship for Leutze, 127
  portrait by Leutze, 128
Abstract art, 151
Academy of the Fine Arts, at Philadelphia, The Pennsylvania, 168
Achenbach, Andreas, 44, 112, 131
Achievements of Leutze in Rome, 39
Adams, Owen, 157
Alaska Purchase, painting of, 136
Alexander, James, 63
Allen, Josephine L., 162
Allston, Washington, 8
American Army, 56, 69, 89, 95
American art, 119–120
American Crisis, The, 70, 94
American flag in the painting, 109–110
American Legion, The, 165, 169
American Revolution, 6, 10, 12
  army of, 62, 65, 69–70, 85, 88
  attack on Trenton, 93–104
  backdrop for the painting, 55, 59
  Battle of Long Island, 56–59
  British advance in fall of 1776, 62, 67
  British arrival in summer of 1776, 56

American Revolution—(*Continued*)
  conference at Thompson-Neely House, 89–92
  Delaware crossing plans, 72–86
  Europe, loss of faith in, 75–76
  Hessians in, 56, 61, 73, 81, 95, 101–102
  Washington's strategy, 58, 67, 81, 89
Ancestors depicted in the painting, 107
Apollo Association, 34
Army hospitals, 85, 93–94
Arnold, Richard James, 34
Arrival of the painting at site, 161–168
Art commissions in Fredericksburg, 17
Artists' Fund Society, exhibits in, 1, 28, 36
  other exhibitors, 22
  sponsor, 23
Assunpink Creek, 102
"Atheneum Portrait," 48
Atkinson, J. Beavington, 31
Atlantic, first crossing of, 13

Ballad on Delaware Crossing sung at festival, 20–21
Barker, Captain A. S., 141
Battle, of Chancellorsville, 133
  of Long Island, 57–59
  of Trenton, 12, 101–102, 103, 128–129
Bayard, John, 75
Beaumont's Ferry, 89
Benjamin, Samuel, 149

183

Bethlehem, army hospital at, 85
Betsy Ross house, 11
Bierstadt, Albert, 43
Birch, Thomas, 23
Birthplace of Leutze, 3
Blunt, Captain John, 99
Boat, occupants of the, 107, 109
Bonaparte, Charles J., 142
Bontzolakis, Dr. Elie, on abstract art, 151
Boston Museum of Fine Arts, 121
Bowman's Hill, 75, 80, 83, 91
Boy Scouts of America, 165, 169
Bremen canvas, the, 113
Briggs, John, 52
Bristol, 97, 98, 99
British troops, flight of, after Delaware Crossing, 103
    landing of, in New York, 56
    plans of, to cross Delaware, 81
    prisoners sent to Philadelphia, 103
Bryant, Louisa Munson, 45
Bucks County Federation of Women's Clubs, 79, 168
Burk, The Reverend Herbert, 157
Burroughs, Bryson, 152
Butcher, Dr. Borton, 89

Cadena, Luis, 48
Cadwalader, Colonel John, 73, 97, 98, 99
Canova, Antonio, 121
Capitol, first commission for, 122
    last commission for, 137
    mural for, 125
    paintings in, 9
    reception at, 2
    "Washington Crossing the Delaware" in, 112, 113, 114
Carey, Edward L., 23, 28, 40
Ceremony at Crossing, 169–170
Children, Leutze's, 123
Christmas celebration, Fredericksburg, 20–21
Cigrand, Dr. Bernard J., 147
Cioppa, Prudence della, 175–176
Civil War, 129, 133–134

Clay, Henry, 123
Coffin, William Sloane, news release on the painting, 155
Colonial Dames of America, The, 170
Columbianum, The, 8
Columbus, paintings on, 27, 33, 34, 36, 39, 45
Common Sense pamphlets, 70
Comstock, Dr., 28
Confederate hold on ports, 134
Congress, commissions art works, 122–123
    flight to Baltimore in 1776, 72, 73
Continental Army, 62, 65, 69–70, 88
Controversies over painting, 40, 110, 146–147, 169
Cooper, Senator James, 116, 122
Cooper, William, 166
Corcoran, W. W., 123, 124
Corcoran Art Gallery, 52, 123
Cornwallis, Lord, 62, 66, 70–71
Coryell's Ferry, 89
Councils of War, 1776, 81, 83, 92
Crossing of the Delaware, British plans, 81
    final plans, 97–100
    Stirling's role in, 77
    Washington's strategy, 80–81, 89
Custis, George Washington Parke, 48

Darragh, Lydia, 12
Daughters of the American Revolution, The, 52–53, 165, 169
Defense line along the Delaware, 89
DeForest, Robert W., 153
DeLacey, Donald, 53
Delaware River, condition of, 97, 99
    crossing plans, 77, 78, 80–81, 97–100
    scene of portrait, 56
Demont, William, traitor, 61

184

Descendants of the Signers of the Declaration of Independence, 170
Design for U.S. stamp, 35
DeStoeckel, Baron, 136
Dickinson, General Philemon, 89
Dohanos, Stevan, 176
Dred Scott Decision, 125
Dunk's Ferry, 89
Durand, Ashur, 124
Durham boats, used in crossing, 71, 98, 99, 109, 167
Düsseldorf, education in, 27–35
portraits made in, 45
return to, 42, 123
Düsseldorf School of Painters, 29, 150

Easby, Dudley T., Jr., 163
Eaton, The Reverend Jesse, 167
Education in Europe, 27–35
Eighth Virginia Regiment, 5
Ellis, F., 35
Entry room, of Thompson-Neely House, *illus.*, 79
Ewing, Brigadier General James, 97, 99
Exhibit problems at church, 163–164

Fairman, Charles E., 112, 120
Family of Leutze, 23
Faraday, Michael, 13
Federation of Women's Clubs, 173
Fee for Capitol mural, controversy over, 126–127
Fermoy, M. A., 88
Field, John W., 28
Figures in the painting, 107, 110–112
Financial problems of Leutze, 22, 26, 30
First art commission, Leutze's, 122
First railroad line in U.S., 13
Fisher, Norman, 173, 174
Flag in the painting, controversy over, 109–110
Fort Lee, evacuation of, 62, 65

Fort Washington, N. Y., loss of, 65
retreat to, 61
Franklin, Benjamin, 12, 93
Franklin Institute, 8
Fredericksburg, life in, 16–21
French and Indian War, 63

Gates, General Horatio, 76, 99
Gebell, Julia Leutze, 24
German-American Colonists, 5–6
German "models" repudiated, 110–112, 147–148
Germany, 19th-century, 3–4
Leutze's return to, 41, 131
Gillam, A. Henry, Jr., 168
Girl Scouts, 169
Glover, Colonel John, 59, 91, 99
Gmünd, 3, 6, 36
God, Robert E., 156
Goupil and Vibert, purchasers of the painting, 114, 115, 122, 145
Grant, General James, 78, 88
Grant, General Ulysses S., 135
Graves of Unknown Soldiers, *illus.*, 96
Greene, General Nathanael, 56, 61, 81, 92
Gridley, Captain Richard, 75
Grundy, Senator Joseph R., 164

Haddonfield Chapter, D.A.R., 174
"Hagar and Ishmael," first canvas, 17
Hale, Edward Everett, 129
Hale, Nathan, 60–61
Hamilton, Captain Alexander, 68, 91, 92
Harlem Heights, 60, 86
Harmon, Patricia, 177
Havemeyer, H. O., 152
Hawthorne, Nathaniel, 135
Hayes, Helen, visitor to Park, 173
"Head" of Washington, 52, 53
Helms, Charles B., 157
Hessians, arrival of, 56
attack Fort Washington, 61–62
defeat of, 101–102

185

Hessians—(*Continued*)
  outrages of, 83
  at Trenton, 81, 95, 102
Hill, Mrs. Jane Jordan, 107
Historic Philadelphia sites, 12
Holiday, story of painting, 146
Honeyman, John, spy, 82
Hooker, General Joseph, 133
Houdon, Jean Antoine, bust of Washington, 50
  mask used by Leutze, 50–51, 52, 155
Howe, Admiral Lord Richard, 56, 58, 59
Howe, Sir William, 56, 60, 61
Hudson River School, 44, 45, 149
Hughes, Rupert, 150
Humphrey, Lieut. Winslow, 146
Huntington, Daniel, 39
Hutchinson, Mrs. Joseph B., 157

Ingersoll, J. R., 36
Inman, Henry, 8
International Business Machines Corp., owner of painting, 113
Irving, Washington, 135
Isham, Samuel, 151
Italy, Leutze's work in, 36–39

Johnson, Eastman, 44, 105
Jordan, Josiah, 107

Kennedy, John S., 145, 146, 150
Kent, Henry W., 110, 153
Knights of Pythias, 169
Knox, Colonel Henry, 91, 92
Knyphausen, Wilhelm von, 56, 61

Landstrom, Russell, 147
Lee, General Charles, 67, 76, 77, 80
Lee, General Robert E., 129
Leslie, Charles R., 41
Lessing, Karl Friedrich, 31, 44
Letters, Leutze's, 13, 15, 16, 18, 21, 22, 23, 24, 26, 29, 30, 42
Leutze, Catherine, 43, 133

Leutze, Cornelia Buckley, 43
Leutze, Emanuel Gottlieb, Alaska painting, 136
  artistic development, 10–11
  Atheneum portrait, 48
  birthplace, 3
  boyhood in Philadelphia, 3, 6, 8, 9
  Bremen canvas, 113
  children, 123
  death, 137–138
  Düsseldorf, 27–35, 42, 45, 123
  early art efforts, 9, 10, 50
  emigrates to America, 5
  Europe, education and work in, 27–39, 40–41
  exhibits at Artists' Fund Society, 1–2, 23, 27, 28
  family, 23
  fee for Capitol mural, 126–127
  financial problems, 22, 26, 30
  first commission, 22
  in Fredericksburg, 17
  Germany, return to, 41–42, 131
  "head" of Washington made, 52, 53
  marriage, 24, 42
  newspaper comments on, 138, 154–155
  paintings, titles of, 27, 28, 33, 34, 36, 37, 39, 40, 45, 123–124, 125, 136, 137, 157, 158
  Philadelphia, return to, 26, 118, 120
  portraits of family, 143
  pronunciation of name, 1
  reception in Washington, D.C., 1–2, 9, 13
  romances, 32
  schooling, early, 7
  Virginia, life in, 24
  "Washington Crossing the Delaware," story of, 2, 12, 55, 59, 65, 107, 108, 109, 111–112, 113, 114 (See also separate entry.)
Leutze, Gottlieb, 3–5, 7, 8, 11

Leutze, Henry Eugene Cozzens, 43, 50, 126, 130–131, 134, 139, 140–143
Leutze, Ida, 43
Leutze, Julia, 123, 131
Leutze, Louisa, 22–25
Leutze, Trevor McClurg, 23, 123, 126
Leutze, Trevor William, 143
Lewton, F. L., 35
Library of Congress, fire, 122
Long, John D., 141
Lottner, Julia, 35, 42, 43
Lovett, Caroline Lewis, 50

McCall, P., 23, 36
M'Cormick, H., 28
McKonkey's Ferry, 97, 98
McMurtie, Dr., 28
MacWhorter, Alexander, 67
Maier, Jacob, 4
Map, Trenton and Environs, 54
Marblehead fishermen, 59, 99
Marriage of Leutze, 22, 24, 42
Marshall, Chief Justice John, 55, 87
Martha Washington Garden Club, 168
Martin, Mrs. E. Linton, 91
Mason, William, 28
Maxwell, General, 67
Meade, General George Gordon, 133
Meigs, General Montgomery C., 123
Melhorn, F. Caroline, 174
Mercer, General Hugh, 19, 88, 92
Mercer, Hugh, Jr., 20
Merrick House Conference, 72, 81
Methodist Church at Crossing, 163–168
Metropolitan Museum, acquisition of the painting, 2, 145, 146
    attitude toward painting, 148–150, 152, 153–154
    defense of flag in the painting, 110
    loans the painting, 161–162
Miller, Christina, 4, 11

Miller, Louisa, 11, 23, 24
Mills, Clark, 124
Minor, John, 16, 17, 21
Missouri Compromise, 124
Models chosen for painting, 110, 111–112
Monroe, James, 13, 85–86, 92, 93
Monroe Doctrine, 86
Monticello, blockade runner, 134
Moore, Captain James, death of, 97
Morris, Gouverneur, model for Washington statue, 51
Morris, Robert, 73–74, 81
Morristown, Lord Stirling sent to, 76, 88
Muhlenberg, John, 5, 6
Muhlenberg, Reverend Heinrich, 5, 6
Munich, Leutze's studies in, 35–36
Mural in Capitol, 125–127
Muther, Richard, acclaims the painting, 149

National Academy of Design, 39, 105, 124
Nationalism, stirring of, 13
Neuhaus, Eugene, art critic, 136
Newark, N. J., arrival of Washington, 66–67
New Jersey, British in, 64–66
Newspaper editorials, 138, 154–155
New York City Artists' Fund Society, 133
New York *Herald Tribune*, report on the painting, 154
New York Metropolitan Fair, 128
New York Times, The, report on ceremony, 170
Nicaragua Expedition, 139
"Norseman" canvas, criticism, 40–41
North Carolina rejects Sully work, 121

Okie, J. B., 28
Old Ferry Inn, *illus.*, 106
Otis, Bass, 65

187

Owners of Leutze paintings, list of, 28, 36

Paine, Thomas, 70
"Paintbox, The," German artists' club, 123
Paintings, titles of Leutze's, 27, 28, 33, 34, 36, 37, 39, 40, 45, 123–124, 125, 136, 137, 157, 158
Panama Canal, 140
Panic of 1837, 15, 18
Parents, Leutze's, 3, 4, 5, 7, 8, 11
Patriotic Order of Sons of America, 169
Peale, Charles Willson, 8
Peale, Rembrandt, 23
Peale, T. R., 124
Pease, Murray, 161–162, 163
Pennsylvania Academy of the Fine Arts, The, 8, 53
Philadelphia, attack planned, 73
  in Leutze's day, 6–8, 12
  Leutze's return to, 26, 118, 120
  retreat to, 66
Philadelphia Free Library, Washington portrait in, 50
Philadelphia *Inquirer*, editorial, 158
Philadelphia *Record*, editorial, 157–158
Phelon, Henry A., 134
Phillips, H. I., 154
Point of Embarkation, 159
Poor, Rear Admiral C. H., 139
Portraits, first fees for, 113
  of family, 143
Princeton, 68, 71, 104
"Protection papers," 82–83
Putnam, Israel, 56–57, 58, 97, 99
Pennsylvania, Army crosses to, 71
Pierce, Franklin, 123

Railroad, first, 13
Rall, Colonel Johann, 78, 97–101
Redfield, E. W., 53
Revolution as backdrop for the painting, 55
Richardson, E. P., 120
Rittenhouse, David, 73

Roberts, Marshall O., 145
Romances, Leutze's, 32
Romantic Movement in Europe, 33
Rome, Leutze in, 39
Roosevelt, Franklin Delano, 152, 156
Roosevelt, Theodore, 142
Rorimer, James J., 159
Rosin, Harry, 53
Rowcliff, Marian Leutze, 143
Rowcliff, Rear Admiral Gilbert J., 143
Rush, Dr. Benjamin, 69

St. Clair, Brigadier General Arthur, 102
St. Gaudens, Homer, 153
Sartain, John, 26
Saturday Evening Post, 176
Schadow, Friedrich Wilhelm, 31
School attendance at Crossing Park, 174–177
Schwartze, George, 23
Scott, O. M., 113
Seward, William H., 125, 130
Sheldon, Elisha, 67
Shirley, General William, 63
Sill, Joseph, 36
Sketches for painting, 47, 105
Slidell, John, 133–134
Smallwood, Colonel William, 57
Smith, Mrs. Charles Harper, 167, 168
Snider, Jacob, Jr., 28
Snyder, G. W., 36
Society of the Cincinnati, 19
Sons of the American Revolution, 169
Sons of the Revolution, 169
South, position of, 134
South Amboy, British flight to, 103
Stamp, Columbian Series, 35
Stanton, Edwin M., 129
Stark, Colonel John, 91
State requests for painting, 156–157
S.S. *Tallahassee*, 134
Stelwagon, Charles K., 23, 50

Stephen, General Adam, 88
Stirling, General Lord, Battle of Long Island, 57
  career of, 62–65
  at Council of War, 91
  errand to Morristown, 76–78
  illness, 85, 88
  role in Revolution, 62
Stone, Horatio, 124
Story, Justice Joseph, 87
Stradling, Granville, 166
Stuart, Gilbert, 8, 48–50, 119
Sullivan, General John, 56, 58, 92
Sully, Thomas, 8, 23, 121
Swedish Museum, Philadelphia, 113

Talbot House, Philadelphia, 35
Tallmadge, Colonel Benjamin, 58
Taney, Chief Justice Roger B., 124, 125
Taylor, Francis Henry, 162
Taylor, Myron C., 146, 158
Taylor, Samuel, 163
Taylorsville, 24, 163
Terhune, Abram, 107
Terhune, Albert Payson, 107
Test, Mary Ann, 175
Texas, painting on loan in, 162, 165
Third Virginia Regiment, 102
Thirteenth Regiment, Motto, 95
Thompson-Neely House, 74, 75, 79, 80, 82, 83, 84, 86, 90, 164
  scene of council, 89–93
Time Magazine, report on the painting, 2
Titles of Leutze's paintings, 27, 28, 33, 34, 36, 37, 39, 40, 45, 123–124, 125, 136, 137, 157, 158
Towne, John, 36, 41
Trenton, advance on, 101
  attack, plans for, 72, 77–78, 93
  map, 54
  victory at, 102
Trenton Falls, 98
Trevelyan, Sir George Otto, 104
Trumbull, Colonel John, 8, 9

Trumbull, Governor Jonathan, of Connecticut, 49, 75
Tuckerman, Henry T., 40–41, 116
Turner, Dr. Henry W., 169

Underwood, Bold, Spencer and Hufty, 26
Uniforms, details of in the painting, 109, 111–112
Union Blockade, 134

Valley Forge, 103
Venetian School of painting, 37
Venice, Leutze in, 37
Versions of famous canvas, 113–114
Veterans of Foreign Wars, 169
Virginia, Leutze in, 24
Visitors to Crossing Park, record of, 171–174
Von Dechow, Friedrich, 102
Von Donop, Colonel Carl, 97

Walter, Thomas U., 123
War Act for Defense, 142–143
Washington Art Association, 124
Washington Bicentennial, 154–155, 156, 158, 159
Washington, W. D., 124
Washington, Captain William, 86
Washington Crossing, 72, 163
Washington Crossing Memorial Building, 159
Washington Crossing Park Commission, 2, 53, 159, 167, 170
Washington Crossing State Park, 75, 97
  celebration, 1952, 168–170
  illustration, 106
  painting at, 147
  visitors' record, 171–174
"Washington Crossing the Delaware" (painting):
  ancestors in, 107
  arrival at site, 161–168
  in Capitol, 114
  controversies, 40, 65, 110, 146–147, 154–155, 169

"Washington Crossing the Delaware" (painting) (*Cont.*):
damage by fire (first version), 113
defense of, 157–158
exhibit problems at Park, 163–164
history of, 2, 12, 55, 59
message of, 177
Metropolitan Museum controversy, 152, 154–155
occupants of boat, 65, 107, 109
sale of at auction, 145
size of canvas, 108
State requests for, 168–170
tributes to, 116–119
versions of, 113, 114
Washington Bicentennial celebration, 156–157
Washington's figure in, 108, 109, 111–112
Washington, D.C., Leutze in, 2, 13, 14, 15, 16
Washington, George, 6, 11, 12, 165
attack on Trenton, 93–104
Battle of Long Island, 56–59
changes defensive pattern, 89
character of, as model, 46–47
conception of, in the painting, 108–109, 111–113
conference at Thompson-Neely House, 89–92
at Council of War, 92

Washington, George—(*Continued*)
Delaware Crossing plans, 67, 71, 72–86, 97–100
determination of, 100
"head" of, by Leutze, 53
Houdon bust and mask, 50–52
immortalized by Leutze, 117
leadership qualities, 55, 66–67
market for paintings of, 49–50
plans for action, 68, 70–71
statue rejected, 121
strategy of, 58, 60, 88, 89
Washington, William, 91
Washington's Birthday celebration, 1952, 168–170
Weedon, George, 19, 20, 60
Weir, Robert W., 124
West, Benjamin, 8
"Westward the Course of Empire Takes Its Way," mural in Capitol, 125–126
White Plains, attack on, 61
Whittridge, Euphemia, 107, 155
Whittridge, Worthington, 44, 105, 107, 110–111, 148, 149–150
Williams, T. Harry, 129
Württemberg, 3
Wynne, Thomas Elliott, 168

Yardley Methodist Church, 163
Yorktown, 104

Zenger, Peter, 63

190